ROLE RECONSIDERED
a re-evaluation of the relationship
between teacher-in-role and acting

ROLE RECONSIDERED
a re-evaluation of the relationship between teacher-in-role and acting

Judith Ackroyd

Trentham Books

Stoke on Trent, UK and Sterling, USA

Trentham Books Limited
Westview House   22883 Quicksilver Drive
734 London Road   Sterling
Oakhill   VA 20166-2012
Stoke on Trent   USA
Staffordshire
England ST4 5NP

First published 2004

British Library Cataloguing-in-Publication Data
A catalogue record for this book is available from the British
Library

1 85856 310 0

Cover photographs by Tim Halliday.

Designed and typeset by Trentham Print Design Ltd., Chester
and printed in Great Britain by Cromwell Press Ltd., Wiltshire.

Contents

For
my brother, Jeremy

ACKNOWLEDGEMENTS

I am indebted to David Booth, Simon Callow, Jonothan Neelands, Fiona Shaw, Joe Winston and especially Cecily O'Neill and John O'Toole for giving me time and support while I was preparing the work for this book. I also wish to thank Gavin Bolton, Dorothy Heathcote, Norah Morgan, Juliana Saxton, Philip Taylor and the many others who have shared their ideas in published form and have therefore helped me further my understanding of drama in education. I hope I am forgiven for picking and poking at the writing of others and that I will remember to forgive those who do the same with this text to continue to generate a better grasp of the extraordinary phenomenon of teacher-in-role!

This book provides an opportunity to thank David Davis for the remarkable preparation he gave me on the PGCE in Drama in Education at what was then Birmingham Polytechnic over twenty years ago. (My dissertation was 'Teacher-in-role: Tool or Technique?' I clearly haven't moved on, David!). I also wish to acknowledge the professional support and happy friendship Ian Spiby has given me over the last eleven years at UCN. Thank you, Gillian Klein at Trentham Books, for your trust and for the contract!

I wish to thank dear friends new and old for their love, support and friendship, particularly Mick, Joey, Andy, Kerry, Aidan, Erica, John, Ian McC, Carol, Harvey, the 'over the hill club' and Johan. It has been a privilege and such fun to have been born into the family that is mine. Not only a great childhood, but a great present, too. Thanks to you all – Mum and Dad, Jeremy, aunts and uncles and cousins. I have even been spoiled with a wonderful 'second' family, too. Jess and Chad, you always turned up with wine when writing was slowing down...or did it slow down because you turned up with wine?

Toby and Rupert, 'You are the sunshine of my life' (This is the title of a song sung by Stevie Wonder, famous in the olden days when I was in my teens)

Andy, my wonderful husband, thanks for all you have given me. 'You're my Napoleon brandy', not to mention my coliseum! With love.

Definitions – and thinking about definitions – are valuable and essential, but they must never be made into absolutes; if they are, they become obstacles to the organic development of new forms, experiment and invention. It is precisely because an activity like drama has fluid delimitations that it can continuously renew itself from sources that had hitherto been regarded as lying beyond its limits. (Esslin, 1978, p11)

INTRODUCTION
POSING THE QUESTION:
IS TEACHER-IN-ROLE ACTING?

In the spring of 1998 I delivered a paper with Andrew Pilkington, a sociologist, at an international drama conference in Cork. I worked as a teacher-in-role in our presentation to provide the context for our research. Immediately after the paper, a drama education practitioner noted that I was clearly a teacher working in role, and not an actor, citing the way I had dealt with some late arrivals to prove his point. Later that day an actor approached me and said that it was interesting to see another actor at the conference.

This struck me powerfully as I had always assumed that working in role as a teacher was not the same as acting. I was left wondering what it is that we do as teachers in role. Am I an actor when I work in role? Is role-taking different from acting? What does taking on role actually involve?

> One can work for years [says Barba] behind a door with the word 'Theatre' written on it. All that you do requires a meaning so that your work seems justified. But what happens when the door and its sign is knocked down? (Roose-Evans, 1999, p173)

My sign, in Eugenio Barba's construct, had been 'teacher-in-role-not acting'. Now my door and sign had been knocked down.

★★★

In 'Richard II', I'm standing there, facing the audience, saying, 'I'm pretending to be Richard II, and you're going to pretend that I'm Richard II, okay? That's what we're going to play. So I'm starting now!' (Shaw, cited in Zucker, 1999)

I find this fascinating as it is reminiscent of my early teacher roles with classes I did not know or with whom I did not feel secure. 'Please accept me in this role. Please speak to me as if I am a traffic warden!' 'Don't tell me that space travellers don't wear skirts and beads!' Fiona Shaw was anxious because it was the first time she had played a male role, and it was a king, and it was the National Theatre. Both of us knew that nothing could be achieved if those sharing our spaces (whether auditorium or classroom) would not or could not pretend with us.

The actor and audience give mutual consent to sharing in a pretend. No one needs to believe that Fiona Shaw is King Richard, nor I the space traveller. They just have to agree that Shaw speaks as if she is Richard and I speak as if I am the space traveller.

Just as Shaw felt that Deborah Warner's experimental production had a risk element, I have been one of those teachers Fleming talks about who has 'been faced by pupils who fail to take their efforts seriously [and can] attest to the fact that the technique [of teacher working in role] is not without its risks either' (1997).

Four years ago I would never have dreamed of making such a comparison. What I did in role in the classroom bore no relation to what an actor did on the stage. Yet, the experience at Cork made me think that it was time to look more closely.

Re-considerations

The title of this book, *Role Reconsidered*, through its implicit reference to Philip Zarrilli's edited book on acting, (*Acting (Re)Considered*, 1996) self-consciously invites a connection to be made between the field of drama education and the world of performance. It is this connection which is at the heart of my journey. To discover if teacher-in-role is acting I have to explore notions of acting. Zarrilli's collection of essays are written from many different perspectives and raise issues that are relevant to a (re)consideration of teacher-in-role. In his introduction, the first point Zarrilli draws our attention to is the rift between theorists and practitioners:

There are many languages and discourses of acting, each written/spoken from a particular point of view. Theorists often speak only to theorists; practitioners only to practitioners. Too seldom do they speak to each other and to those parts of our 'selves' which might practice theory or theorise practice. (1996, p1)

The same has not really been the case in the field of drama in education, which has continued to develop its theory alongside its practice. Those who have influenced theory have usually influenced practice and visa versa. However, a particular communication gap in the field of drama education emerges, as there seems to have been very little talking between teachers and actors. I propose that in the field of drama education a series of assumptions have been made about acting behaviour, but a richer understanding of acting processes has rarely been sought through connection with actors. As Zarrilli seeks to bridge a gap, so this text will address a gap I perceive in the field.

Zarrilli 'invites the reader to (re)consider both acting and discourses on acting.' This text will attempt to provide a taste of this, alongside a detailed reconsideration of teacher role and discourses on teacher role. He uses '(re)consider [as opposed to reconsider] to mark clearly the implicitly processual nature of 'considering" (1996, p1). We can acknowledge only temporary understandings since the processes do not stop, and theatre and drama emerge and re-emerge, shifting and reforming. Our understandings of theatre do not stand still. There are two major explanations for this. Firstly, the object for consideration keeps changing: performance experiments are constantly underway, new styles develop and conventions are continually broken. Secondly, our way of looking at theatre and performance continually changes, partly due to the changes mentioned above, but also as new theoretical perspectives are applied to the field.

In the light of such constant changes, I wish to echo Zarrilli's sense of process, but in the field of drama education. There is a developing body of literature, and practice continues to evolve. Any proposals about teacher-in-role that may be articulated in this text are modestly made as temporary understandings, subject to the same evolution of ideas and practices as theatre. *Acting (Re)Considered* identifies theatre-making as 'a socio-cultural practice'. As such it is not 'an innocent or naive activity separate from or above and beyond everyday reality, history, politics, or economics' (p1). This is as relevant to theatre making in the classroom as it is to professional theatre. In this book I take it as given that the improvisational event of teacher working in role in a classroom cannot be isolated from the particular drama form, its time, place and context.

Arguably, one of the strengths of the field of drama in education continues to be its capacity and willingness to re-evaluate its practices and investigate and reposition theoretical assertions. Historically there are many examples of this. Since 'Slade burst on to the scene at the Bonnington conference in 1948 with the claim that child drama is different to theatre' (Davis, 1998, pxi) the relationship between theatre and drama in education has been often reconsidered. By 1980 Ken Robinson described Dorothy Heathcote as seeing no 'dichotomy between theatre and drama activities in education.' (p3). *In Structuring Drama Work* (1990) Jonothan Neelands used the terms *theatre* and *drama* synonymously, and five years later Cecily O'Neill described process drama as a *theatre event* (1995a). Fleming in 1997 explained that 'Publications on drama now largely take it for granted that the dichotomies between 'process' and 'product'; 'theatre' and 'drama'; 'drama for understanding' and 'drama as art'; 'experience' and 'performance' were false dichotomies' and goes on to summarise some of the reasons for the new consensus (p1-2).

Gavin Bolton's *Acting in Classroom Drama* (1998) looks at widely held views leading to a call for a broader perspective on what it is that children are doing in classroom drama. He searches 'for a generic unity between what has been central to his teaching, the value of dramatic playing... and other forms of acting behaviour' (Davis, 1998, px). Bolton's purpose in the book is to .

> give the term 'acting' serious consideration ... [He uses] drama exponents' implicit or explicit perceptions of acting behaviour as a basis for a revised conceptual framework. This reformulation attempts to make a case for embracing, in the classroom,

many different kinds of acting behaviour as a basis that go
beyond the limits and responsibilities of a stage actor, while
nevertheless including both 'stage' acting and that kind of acting behaviour associated with 'teacher-in-role' led drama.
(Bolton, 1998, pxvii)

But there is a lacuna here. Bolton in his reconsideration has not reconsidered the role of the teacher. Nor, indeed, has anyone else.
The teacher-in-role continues to be identified as something other
than acting. If we have an understanding of the teacher taking part
in the drama with the children (who are acting), why isn't the
teacher acting, too?

I want to investigate the teacher-in-role and see if that, too, cannot
be included in what Bolton calls *acting behaviour*. Is the teacher-in-
role acting? If not, what is she doing? If she is acting, what sort of
acting is it? With which acting traditions can it be identified? I too,
wish to use 'drama exponents' implicit or explicit perceptions of
acting behaviour as a basis for a revised conceptual framework'
(*ibid*). It may engage us in a broadening of our concept of acting
and it might also engage us in a new notion of teacher-in-role. The
desire to broaden concepts of acting is central to Zarrilli's volume.
He

invites students of acting, actors, and theorists alike to put aside
parochial preconceptions and points of view that propose
acting as a truth (that is, one system, discourse, or practice).
(He) invites instead a pro-active, processual approach which
cultivates a critical awareness of acting as multiple and always
changing. (1996, p3)

If 'acting' covers such a huge range of activities, I wish to consider
whether the teacher-in-role might be appropriately included among
them.

My context

I was introduced to the practice of teacher-in-role during my post-
graduate teacher training course with David Davis at the University of Central England in Birmingham over twenty years ago. It
was taught as a crucial pedagogic strategy for the drama teacher.
All the student teachers used it in their practice. My dissertation,

entitled 'Teacher-in-role: Tool or Technique?' took it as its focus. Drama had been a subsidiary subject in my first degree and I had had some experience of acting, but I embraced teacher-in-role as something very different. I thoroughly enjoyed working in role and was convinced of its efficacy, so that some years later when I joined an advisory service I eagerly introduced teachers to the practice.

During those years and more recently when training teachers, I continued to argue that working in role was not the same as acting. It was not just that I figured this would make the task less daunting for teachers or students who had not studied drama. I did firmly believe that the two were distinctly different. However, other parts of my teaching seem to have assumed a close relationship between acting and teacher-in-role. Whilst saying it was different on the one hand, I was on the other hand teaching students how to draw on their understanding of kinetics and proxemics when taking roles. Familiarity with semiotics' texts such as *Theatre as a Sign System* (Aston and Savona, 1991) and Pavis' questionnaire (1985, p208-12) were compulsory. The education students were obliged to video themselves teaching to enable them to analyse their drama lessons in relation to a host of criteria, but particularly to see how they signed in role to the children in role. Were they giving cross messages through words and body language? Were the gestures too big so that they inhibited the children's participation? Did the role provide an appropriate model for the children to follow? Was the integrity of the role apparent?

About four years ago my teaching commitment at work changed from teacher training courses to drama courses. I now work in the drama department of a division of Performance Studies. Looking back, this change coincided with my re-think about the activity of teacher-in-role. Our drama students are required to consider the semiotic aspects of performances and we expect them to under-stand how communication is made through signing systems such as tone of voice and gesture. I am left wondering if the questions I asked the education students about how they signed in role were significantly different from the questions I now ask drama students about an actor's performance.

Mapping this book

This book has two inter-linked sections. Section One begins with a look at the common assumptions about teacher-in-role's difference from acting. It then examines the key points that are seen to create that difference, with consideration of the literatures of drama in education and the fields of performance and theatre. Bringing together these two literatures created an interesting defamiliarisation process that allowed me to analyse familiar literature in the field of drama in education through a new perspective. Through this process, the differences conceived between teacher-in-role and acting seem to disappear. The final chapter of Section One considers the assumptions that appear to have underpinned thinking about teacher-in-role and why they may have been maintained. Section Two looks at a sample of the work of educational practitioners Cecily O'Neill and John O'Toole and actor Fiona Shaw, in three case studies. Each investigates one observation of practice, an interview and analysis of these in the light of the theoretical considerations of Section One. Can theories and categories usually applied to performance be used to examine and categorise teacher-in-role? The answer, we'll find, is yes. Were the approaches and skills used by the actor different from those of the teachers? The answer, we'll find, is no.

The journey through both sections refuses to be uncomplicated mainly due in the first section to the instability of concepts, and in the second to lack of existing frameworks with which to examine teacher-in-role. Let us briefly consider both.

Looking at what has been written about role and acting inevitably leads to problems with regard to definitions and implications. Language and definitions are slippery and what we once assumed were shared views are not necessarily shared. Lyotard suggests that 'truth claims' and assumed consensus of universal history are now untenable (Selden and Widdowson, 1993, p184). He argues that the 'grand narrative has lost its credibility' (Lyotard, 1984) and identifies as part of postmodernism a destabilising of assumptions and a 'relentless critique of the legitimacy of any form of social or ideological meaning' (Easthope and McGowan, 1992, p183). Here we can identify the spirit of Zarrilli's collection in which only temporary conceptualisations are sought. Given that postmodernism is frequently identified with a 'generalised pessimism about the possibility of social change' (Fortier, 1997, p120), let us pick up on Lyotard's identification of a positive advantage in the postmodern commitment to critiquing the legitimacy of assumptions. Communities have built up their own histories and sets of assumptions, and have mutually supported these narratives. We will find examples in the field, or 'community' of drama education that are significant to this study.

Turning to the case studies: I wanted to construct a model to enable a systemised analysis of practice in order to investigate both theory and practice. There is no precedent for analysing teacher-in-role in relation to acting, so I constructed a semiotic model. There are limitations to this model as there are limitations to semiotics as a mode of interpretation, but it enabled me to look at the practice of the teachers in role and the actor in exactly the same way. This process is described in chapter 8.

The conclusion brings together the discoveries of the case studies and makes direct comparisons between the practice of both teachers and actor. Issues the work has raised are listed and responses given to key questions, such as:

Is the teacher-in-role acting?

Why does it matter whether teacher-in-role is acting or doing something else?

If we call it acting, how might this affect our practice?

This book offers no final certainties but it does propose a new perspective for viewing the teacher-in-role that will hopefully open up new dialogues, draw upon acting practices to further the exploration of teacher-in-role and suggest some possible implications on practice in the classroom.

Reading this book

Readers may choose different routes through this text. The order presented here involves a sense of development, since the theoretical considerations of Section One are applied to the practice examined in Section Two, and the conclusion derives from all that has pre-

ceded it. However, some readers may wish to look at the conclusions in the final chapter first, and then look back to see how
they were conceived. Those of you who are familiar with the work
of the case study practitioners may choose to read about their
samples of practice in Section Two before returning to Section
One. Teachers may wish to read the session details of O'Neill and
O'Toole and teach them themselves before returning to this text.

SECTION ONE
DESTABALISING DISTINCTIONS
AND DEFINITIONS

1
TEACHER-IN-ROLE AND ACTING AS OPPOSITIONS

Before I embarked on this project, I made a preliminary list of questions I wished to answer by the end of my research. The first two questions were:

- What is the distinction between teacher-in-role and acting?

- What are the commonalities between teacher-in-role and actor-in-role?

These questions assume a neat uncomplicated approach to the inquiry. The last two questions on the list were:

- Is it possible to identify a consensus of what teachers and actors believe they are doing in role?

- Is there enough of a consensus to compare?

On day one I asked 'What is the distinction...?' By the end of three days, I had begun to wonder whether there would even be a consensus with which to make a comparison. This shift from neat categories to the blurring of hard distinctions that emerged during those three days through my list of questions, was a microcosm of what was to follow over the next three years. This section explores the destabalising of distinctions and definitions.

The canonical texts of drama in education tend to point to a distinction between teacher-in-role and acting, as we shall see later in this section. However, when I have worked in role with teachers who do not know me, I have sometimes been asked what kind of acting work I usually do, which suggests that they do not see a difference. Unsure whether the distinctions between concepts of teacher-in-role and acting were confined to the literature or held by the average teacher, I asked a group of teachers who used teacher-in-role, but were not trained in drama, to list features of each practice under two headings. The grid opposite sets out the results.

Taking this grid at face value I could believe my initial question answered: *what is the distinction between teacher-in-role and acting?* The two activities are distinguished on many counts and look very different. However, on close examination it can be seen that the features listed under 'actor' are associated with the dominant Western model of theatre, despite the fact that this is not representative of all actors' work. So there seems to be consensus within the field of drama in education that acting is a very particular activity which is set in opposition with that of teacher-in-role.

Saussure argued that 'the very concepts a language expresses are also defined and determined by its structure. They exist, not intrinsically, as themselves... and not positively, by their actual content, but negatively, by their formal relations with other terms in the structure' (Hawkes, 1977, p28). Hence oppositions are identified which mean that a concept's 'most precise characteristic is in being what the others are not' (Saussure, p117 cited in Hawkes). This structuralist tendency to identify binary oppositions is evident in our simple model above. In order to establish an understanding of teacher-in-role, features describing what it is *not* have been identified, and as we see later in this section, that path all too readily leads to the claim that teacher-in-role is not acting. Territories and boundaries are thus established and the oppositions serve to alienate the possibility of any room between them.

However, I wish to challenge the seeming solidity of these binary oppositions and expose a middle ground from a poststructuralist perspective. The poststructuralists and indeed the postmodernists invite us to conceptualise boundaries as fluid, pointing to the in-

Table 1
CATEGORISING TIR AND ACTOR: THE FIRST MODEL

	Teacher-in-role	Actor
Overall power in the experience	the teacher is privileged	the audience is privileged
Content	chosen by teacher	given to the actor
Intention	to fulfil learning objectives	to entertain
Responsibility for audience welfare and behaviour	fully and legally responsible	no responsibility
Audience attendance	compulsory	voluntary
Audience expectation	to learn (to be bored/ interested?)	to be entertained (to be challenged/ amused?)
Audience role	active participation	inactive participation
Audience relationships	familiar	unfamiliar
Audience size	small group	large group
Audience age	school age	mixed, usually a minority under 25 years
Social class of audience	in state system-mixed, often without upper middle and usually without upper class	predominantly middle class
Selection of role	can be chosen, and can change at any time	given before event and cannot be changed
Response to audience reaction	flexibility to adapt and challenge audience assumptions	no verbal flexibility, no possibility to respond
Environment	school hall/classroom	theatre space

stability of concepts and challenging any sense of the fixed. I seek to illustrate the temporary and unstable nature of definitions and conceptualisations through a critique of the oppositions established, and to propose a more fluid notion of the relationship between teacher-in-role and acting.

2
CHALLENGING THE OPPOSITIONS

It is tempting to begin by defining our key terms. However, this is not easy. In the literature of drama in education, concepts of teacher-in-role are sometimes associated with social roles. At the same time, the role of teaching is itself often taken to entail role taking. It makes it difficult to begin to understand the two as distinct activities. Equally, notions of acting must be considered in relation to performing and to actions of everyday. When John Cage was asked about his definition of theatre, he replied,

> I try to make definitions that won't exclude. I would simply say that theatre is something which engages both the eye and the ear. The two public senses are seeing and hearing ... the reason I want to make my definition of theatre that simple is so one could view everyday life itself as theatre. (cited in M.R. Sandford, 1995, p51)

If theatre is conceived as everyday life, then the role of teacher may be conceived as part of theatre. Where then does this leave an attempt to understand the difference between the role of the teacher and teacher-in-role?

This chapter attempts to interrogate these terms through relating the different fields of literature (drama in education, performance and theatre), and finally proposes that the role of teacher might usefully be identified as performance and that the teacher-in-role seems to fall into many theorists' notion of acting. I am assuming that when we refer to teacher-in-role we mean that the teacher is taking on a role other than herself and working in a fictional context with participants who are usually also in role.

Introducing the complexities

The terms role, performance and acting are used with different connotations in different contexts. We assume that a child ''acting up' means something very different from Fiona Shaw 'acting' Medea convincingly, and that the 'role' of the night club bouncer is different from Shaw getting the lead 'role' of Medea. These distinctions seem fairly obvious at first glance. But, what is the child doing to be described as '*acting up*'? Presumably acting in a particular way that is designed to attract the attention of others and shows an awareness of onlookers and a desire to elicit a particular response; an altered behaviour. Fiona Shaw acting Medea is also doing all of these things. The night club bouncer needs to present himself in a particular way in order to be effective as a bouncer. He will not fulfil his role if he does not look like a bouncer. He cannot look afraid, or those observing him will not believe he could do what a bouncer has to do: deal with the drunk and violent. Fiona Shaw similarly, must present herself in a particular way in order to be effective as Medea. She will not fulfil her role if she does not look appropriate for Medea. She cannot look weak and timid, or those observing her will not believe she could do what Medea has to do: kill the princess and her own two sons. The bouncer is not paid to be stared at. Shaw is. However, he is paid to be seen. Neither bouncer nor child is behaving as if they had different identities, but Fiona Shaw is. However, both child and bouncer may be behaving in a different way from how they would at home with their grandparents. Distinctions are not straightforward.

It is clear why theorists have brought everyday life and acting into the same frame for analysis. Modernity has made us more aware not only that we all play a multitude of roles, but also that some people will go to extraordinary lengths to manage the impressions we have of them. Thus in the 2001 election in Britain the Prime Minister, aware of people's general cynicism towards politics and politicians, deliberately sought to present himself as sincere. In some cases the image may be so successfully portrayed that we are unable to tell the difference between image and reality. This is Baudrillard's nightmare; his vision of 'the generation by models of a real without origin or reality' (Poster, 1988). An example is presented by Inglis:

> President Clinton's appeal to 'my fellow Americans', his warmth and geniality, his sincerity and likeability, attentiveness to others however dim and dull, his suppression of intelligence and fluency, all of which were so brilliantly modelled for him by Robert Redford in the 1972 masterpiece 'The Candidate' (1993, p11).

Schechner points out that 'in the twenty-first century, people as never before live by means of performance' (2002, p22). Schechner, like Goffman, makes no distinction between everyday 'roles' and everyday 'performance'. The terms seem to be used synonymously. Schechner explains that 'Goffman approaches social life as theatre, an interplay of behaviours where players with different motives rehearse their actions, manoeuvre to present themselves advantageously, and often perform at cross purposes with one another. ... people are performing all the time whether or not they are aware of it' (2002, p174).

Teacher-in-role and the role of the teacher

In contrast the field of drama in education makes big distinctions between 'role' and 'performance'. A teacher-in-role is never perceived as a performer. Perhaps performance is construed as too extravagant for the teacher-in-role. Oddly, however, it is not deemed too extravagant for the role of teacher.

'All actions taken by teachers and professionals can be seen as role behaviour. ... The act of teaching confers that professional identity of role upon the incumbent' (O'Hanlon, 1993, p244). Some writers have identified teaching as performing. Whatman's research suggests that 'people with experiences of performing will readily adopt the roles required of teachers because their experiences of performance have taught them the processes of role taking' (1998, p46) and Heck and Williams (1984), Tauber and Mester (1994) and Haigh (1995) all argue that student teachers should be given training in performance skills. Much has been written about this and there is no time here to consider it further, except to note that it seems strange that the role of teacher has been conceived as performing, but never the teacher-in-role used in the drama class. The implication is bizarrely that performance skills are required to be a teacher but not to work in role as a drama teacher. (The skills required for teaching in role are considered in chapter 5.)

It is presumably this sense of performing in everyday life that has led some to seek to identify teacher-in-role as 'social acting'. Toye and Prendiville have attempted to identify the social role of the teacher with the teacher-in-role:

> Looking at 'role' in this sociological rather than theatrical perspective shifts the emphasis away from the skills of the actor in a stage sense to the development of the teacher as a social actor, that is specific semiotic skills appropriate for managing children in the classroom. TiR takes the social actor and the teacher as social actor and puts them in a fictional context. (2000, p52)

While, in the context of their book, the authors are attempting to make working in role appear less daunting for those who are new to it, there is a major problem here. The logical conclusion to this position is that teacher as a social actor in the classroom is doing the same thing as teacher-in-role. If teacher-in-role is simply to be viewed as the social actor in a fictional context, then the creative act most take educational drama to be is denied. The teacher-in-role considers tension, contrasts, the structure and tempo of the drama. Her role is not to use the same gestures in life, since she signs in the language of theatre. Moments are deliberately highlighted in a way they are not in life. Tensions and contrasts are constructed for particular effect in a way they are not in life. Moments are made significant. Bowell and Heap draw the same parallel between social roles and the teacher-in-role, but they see playing a social role as a teacher as a 'small step into teacher-in-role within a process drama' (2001, p49). By identifying the social role that a teacher takes with a teacher-in-role, the artistic function of the teacher-in-role is lost.

Neelands, too, talks of the 'social' actor, which he contrasts with the 'aesthetic' actor. We might expect the teacher to be at the social actor end of the scale and the teacher-in-role at the other. This is not the case. The framework identifies six stages between the social and aesthetic actor for a consideration of students' work (*Beginning Drama*: 11-14 1998a, p17). Neelands explains that

> Students understand from their everyday experience that any social event involves role-taking of some sort...The aesthetic actor builds on this idea of the social actor to create a public role that is a projection of another identity – to behave as Macbeth. (1998, pp15-16)

He is proposing that the social role and the aesthetic role are not completely distinct, but that one is a further development of the other. Returning to our bouncer and Fiona Shaw's performance, he would place the bouncer's performance as social acting and Shaw's as aesthetic. In the six stages, it is not clear how the 'aesthetic' enters the frame, but it is clear that what represents progression through the stages is physical and psychological transformation. The first stage describes social acting when the students act as they would in social situations rather than altering their behaviour for fictional ones. The sixth stage involves significant psychological and physical transformation. If we place the teacher-in-role into this acting framework, it would be most appropriate in stage 3, which describes one who 'begins to imagine, and play with, how someone who is different might respond and behave in the circumstances of the drama' (*ibid* p16). There is a worrying implication here, however, that the teacher-in-role is not working very aesthetically. Because the model has been designed with students' development in mind, it implies that those at earlier stages are not doing the job as well as those at Stage 6 and that further transformation is a more accomplished mode of work. A teacher-in-role would assume a degree of transformation to operate in the fictional context, but would not transform psychologically or physically. So we are left to conclude that teacher-in-role is beyond the social actor but only midway towards the aesthetic actor.

However, the concept of a social/aesthetic continuum takes us a step further in our conceptualisation of teacher-in-role and the role of teacher. The former includes a pretence and includes some degree of 'aesthetic' whereas the role of teacher has no aesthetic (transformation) or fiction. Using this framework for students with teacher-in-role suggests that the teacher-in-role is not simply a social actor.

Many writers seek to highlight ways in which their work in role is different from their work as teacher in the classroom and thereby consider what makes it drama. They refer to features other than transformation. 'Dramatic language is distinguished by the fact that it will always carry more meaning that its obvious surface intentions' (O'Neill, 1995a, p82), just as gestures carry the same extra signification. Language and gesture are read differently in the dramatic context from how they would be in life. So language will be read differently for role of teacher and teacher-in-role. Bolton identifies as an aesthetic aspect of drama work, the 'manipulation of time and space' (1998, p255). What moves the teacher-in-role away from the teacher is the use of theatrical devices. Bolton and Heathcote identify their practice 'as *rooted* in this one artistic characteristic of seeing something as significant. This is essentially the dramatic methodology serving an educational purpose' (their emphasis) (1999, p.ix). The practice of role-playing 'coincides with the essence of theatre. Both are about 'seeing something as significant' (*ibid*). When the teacher-in-role picks up the box that has never been opened, she will handle it differently from the teacher picking up the box. The act is made significant according to the fiction and meanings sought. We will see examples of teachers-in-role making significance in the case studies.

Challenges to notions of acting

We have seen that teacher-in-role cannot be equated with 'social acting'. The teacher-in-role is doing something different from the teacher in her normal role and this difference can be conceived in different ways. Now we turn to destabilising notions of acting.

> I can take any empty space and call it a bare stage. A man walks across this empty space whilst someone else is watching him, and this is all that is needed for an act of theatre to be engaged. (Brook, 1990, p11)

In Brook's familiar description we assume that the man is the actor. Grotowski's aim to strip theatre down to the bare essentials, 'the fundamental encounter between actor and audience' (Neelands and Dobson, 2000, p138) found that all that was necessary was an actor in a space with an audience watching (Grotowski, 1968). However, defining features of theatre and acting have not gone unchallenged. Beckett sought to question the minimal preconditions for performance and 'embarked on a process of aesthetic reduction which culminated in his play *Breath*. *Breath* demonstrates how performance can do without the physical human performer and still constitute a performance' (Hilton, 1987). The piece was very short with a slowly rising curtain, a stage full of rubbish and a baby's cry. After less than a minute, the curtain fell with a dying man's sigh. If *Breath* was theatre, then it challenges Brook's definition. Hilton identifies the pile of rubbish in the same way as he identifies an actor, as an actant. This is an act of designation. Hence, in *Breath*, the three essentials for Hilton are present: space, time and actant. So *Breath* pushes against the familiar definitions of theatre and the assumed role of the actors.

Such experiments to see if assumptions about acting can be dislodged continue. Wilshire describes an extraordinary experience in New York which disrupts our concept of 'the actor, the paradigm of one who stands in for another' (Wiltshire, 1991, pxiii). He went to see a theatre piece entitled *Light Torch* at a warehouse near the docks. The audience were seated and the space darkened.

> In the darkness the main door of the warehouse in the middle of the wall before us slowly rolled up and opened. It went from floor to ceiling and was large enough for trucks to enter and exit. As if surrounded by a nimbus of silence, the sounds of the city could be heard – mostly soft and distant in this area – and cars appeared occasionally, framed by the door, as they passed the street outside. Appeared, but appeared transfigured, as if a spell has been cast over them. (Wilshire, 1991, px)

Trucks reversed into the warehouse and deposited items, such as a sink and an apple, which became 'meaningful in a much more vivid and complete way than they would in ordinary use' (*ibid* pxi). A police car arrived and policemen got out and shone torches up at the audience who laughed a bit. The police, seemingly embarrassed, left. Was this theatre? a space, an audience and people in the space, but those in the space were not party to the theatrical event. They were not conscious of their roles. They constituted actants from the point of view of the spectators and yet what was observed was chance. It was not prepared. The individual trucks and drivers had not been previously designated, but whatever happened to move into the space is inevitably interpreted. Wiltshire describes at length the experience he had.

> We witness theatre experimenting on itself, discovering and underlining the conditions of its own possibility. Its value can be separated out as a factor in any theatre event. 'That is actual things in plain view – not things dressed up or illuminated so as to appear to be what they are not – are nevertheless seen in an entirely new light.' The difference, then, must come from a change in the interpretive attitude of the viewer, not from the things themselves. (*ibid* pxii)

It is an intriguing concept. Watching life positioned as a member of an audience anticipating a theatre event. In this event, there was no one taking on the persona of another which is what we would generally expect from theatre. The actors were not what we think actors should be. Actors are assumed to be other than themselves in the theatrical context and as O'Neill explains, 'all acting is, by definition, unreal' (1995a, p38).

But there are some actors who are working to actually deny any imaginary context or unreality in the theatre. Kirby suggests that

> A difference of opinion has traditionally existed between the 'monists' such as Stanislavsky, who felt that the performer should be unseen within his character, and the 'dualists' such as Vakhtanghov and Brecht, who felt that the performer should be perceived simultaneously with the character so that the one could comment on the other. Now a new category exists in drama, making no use of time, place, or character and no use of the performer's comments. (1987, p7)

He recognises the way in which Happenings have changed our concept of the performer. Handke has experimented with the very conceptual limits of acting. His theatre involves 'speakers' who deliver Handke's lines which have been rehearsed, but they appear as themselves in terms of clothes, hairstyles and voices. 'What the performers say are almost entirely direct statements that would be true no matter who was speaking them. In *Offending the Audience* they speak about the performance situation: 'You are sitting in rows ...You are looking at us when we speak to you ...There is no mirage ... The possibilities of the theatre are not exploited here' (Kirby, 1996, p57).

Handke employs actors to be 'speakers'. They use their own voices, clothes and expressions. Kirby suggests that often 'all' such a performer must do is execute 'a generally simple and undemanding act' (1987, p8). This shifts the source of creativity to the 'artist when he formulated the idea of the action. The performer merely embodies and makes concrete the idea' (*ibid* p8). David Mamet, from a very different tradition, argues that the playwright has the responsibility to create a good play and his description of the actor's role as instrumental. 'The actor is onstage to communicate the play to the audience. That is the beginning and the end of his and her job. To do so the actor needs a strong voice, superb diction, a supple, well proportioned body and a rudimentary understanding of the play' (Mamet, 1997, p9). In contrast to Stanislavski's system, for Mamet the actor's emotions are both irrelevant and dangerous (*ibid* p10).

So actors can be irrelevant for Beckett; untrained, unknown and unaware of their role for Whitman; speaking in denial of a fiction for Handke; and for Mamet the actor's job is to 'show up, and use the lines and his or her will and common sense, to attempt to achieve a goal similar to that of the protagonist" (1997, p12).

The massive range of systems of actor training through the twentieth century (Hodge, 2000) is further evidence of the multiple notions of acting, as is the current lack of conclusion in the United Kingdom drama schools about what students should actually be trained to do. Yoshi Oida crystallises the diversity in describing his experience of working with Peter Brook:

> I realised that I was still performing in accordance with the principles of nōh theatre where the actor's concentration must be extremely intense. But popular theatre requires another approach. And I realised that just as there are many levels of performance, there is no one 'right' way to act. (1992, p72)

John Harrop's book, *Acting*, examines the problem of what it is that actors do (1992). He suggests that an actor is both an artist and an instrument. He sees the playwright writing for an instrument. Over the centuries, this instrument has not really changed (except men acting as women giving way to women acting women), but the way the instrument is used has changed repeatedly and radically. Harrop traces the changes in acting styles and conventions through the ages in British theatre and is interested in the idea of artistry and skill. He identifies contexts in which the actor expects to display her skills as a performer such as the commedia actor, an actor trained in Laban's system, and a contemporary actor in physical theatre. He contrasts this with acting conventions which require the actor to conceal any sign that he is working at the role. The realistic actor is trained to obscure signs of performance. Mamet says, 'I don't care to see a musician concentrating on what he or she feels while performing. Nor do I care to see an actor do so' (p12). The degree to which specific skills are revealed depends to some degree upon the cultural context. Actors trained in kabuki theatre and kathakali, for example, will be trained in specific skills and techniques over years, and audiences will expect to see these exhibited in the performance.

Marvin Carlson identifies a context in which the distinction be-tween the displaying or concealing of skills was crucial to an under-standing of role as distinct from acting. This example is particularly poignant in our quest to understand teacher-in-role and the role of teacher. A couple who are part of a living history project in Fort Ross in Northern Carolina dress in 1830s costumes to greet visitors in their roles as the last Russian commander and his wife. The wife played the piano at one stage to give an 'impression of contemporary cultural life, but later stopped this because she saw it as departing from her role in living history and moving her role into the category of performance. Ms Pritchard did not consider herself 'performing' until she displayed the particular artistic skills needed to give a musical recital' (Carlson, 1998, p3). Carlson sug-gests that despite her personal view, most visitors will assume that she is performing from the moment she first greets them as Elena Rotcheva. Some views of teacher-in-role that we consider in this book suggest that to demonstrate skills could be seen as drawing attention to the teacher, which, as it was for Ms Pritchard, would be seen as inappropriate.

So with assumptions about acting having been extensively challenged, it seems a daunting task to find a way to consider parallels with teacher-in-role.

Acting and performance theory

It is the work of the performance theorists who have developed Goffman's notion of 'performances of everyday life' (1959, p73) and enjoined us to look at the relationship between life and performance differently. The phenomenal growth of experiment has led to a plethora of types of activity that can be labelled performance. After an examination of concepts of performance, acting and their inter-relationships with everyday life enabled me eventually to formulate a theoretical model towards an understanding of everyday life, I will propose a model towards an understanding of everyday life, teacher-in-role and acting.

Richard Schechner highlights the contemporary flux that makes pinning down definitions so very difficult:

> What is a 'performance'? Where does it take place? Who are the participants? Not so long ago these were settled questions, but today such orthodox answers are unsatisfactory, misleading and limiting. 'Performance' as a theoretical category and as a practice has expanded explosively. It comprises a panoply of genres ranging from play, to popular entertainments, to theatre, dance and music, to secular and religious rituals, to 'performance in everyday life', to intercultural experiments and more.' (1996, Editorial Introduction)

In his recent textbook, Schechner attempts an answer to some of these questions:

> Performance must be construed as a 'broad spectrum' or 'continuum' of human actions ranging from ritual, play, sports, popular entertainments, the performing arts (theatre, dance, music), and everyday life performances to the enactment of social, professional, gender, race and class roles, and on to healing (from shamanism to surgery) the media and the internet. Before performance studies, Western thinkers believed

they knew exactly what was and what was not 'performance'. But in fact there is no culturally fixable limit to what is or is not 'performance' ... The underlying notion is that any action that is framed, presented, highlighted, or displayed is a performance. (2002, p2)

This could mean that the work of a silver service waitress could be seen as performance since it is framed by silver service restaurant conventions, such as serving from the left. The elegance of the service system is displayed for the customers who are paying for the ritual. A best man's speech, a lawyer's prosecution and a car sales pitch could all be deemed performance, as could a child persuading a parent for sweets. But what of the classroom teacher? She may well frame and present her lesson in a way that will highlight her learning objectives, and which could be seen as 'displayed as a performance'.

Theorists have sought further distinguishing features. Some have suggested that performing has a consciousness to it (Blau, 1992, Carlson 1996). Clearly, our class teacher has a consciousness of her role and aims in the lesson she is teaching just as she has a consciousness to her teacher-in-role. For Hodge, 'performance' was an appropriate term for stand-up comedians who are not exactly 'acting' yet are playing *consciously* to an audience. Hodge argues that all acting is performance, but not all performance is acting. 'Performing does not have to include 'acting', in that performers can be themselves, and are not pretending or representing anybody else' (2000, p4). So performing has some awareness of audience, but does not necessarily entail impersonation.

This may bring us closer to a concept of performing, but these quotations assume a fixed notion of acting. We now turn to two models of acting proposed by Schechner and Kirby.

For Schechner,

Acting is a sub-category of performing comprising a very broad range of behaviours. At one extreme is the 'minimal acting' of some performance art. At the other extreme is the 'total acting' of shamans and the trance-possessed. Acting consists of focused, clearly marked, and tightly framed behaviours specifically designed for showing. At the non-acting end of the spectrum, there is no portrayal of another or of a character. (2002, p146-7)

So in Schechner's view how is acting distinguished from performing ?

The underlying notion is that any action that is framed, presented, highlighted or displayed is a performance (2002, p2)	Acting consists of focused, clearly marked, and tightly framed behaviours specifically designed for showing (2002, p146-6)

The divide is not all that clear. 'Presented' and 'displayed' meant pretty much the same as 'designed for showing'. Still, it establishes the point that a bricklayer being watched by passersby may be deemed to be a performance although his bricklaying was not specifically designed for showing. We see that acting 'comprises a very broad range of behaviours', from minimal to total.

Minimal acting -- Total acting
(some performance art)   (shamans)

Teacher-in-role might be close to the minimal acting in O'Neill's work (Chapter 9) or further on the continuum towards total acting in some of O'Toole's roles (see chapter 10). Given the pedagogical concerns and responsibilities of care, it is clearly inappropriate for teacher-in-role to be at the total acting position which implies a remove from the concrete reality, the actor being in another state.

Kirby creates a continuum between non-acting and acting (1987, pp3-10). 'In most cases, acting and non-acting are relatively easy to recognise and identify ... But there is a scale or continuum of behaviour involved, and the differences between acting and non-acting may be small' (*ibid* p3). Non-acting is 'where the performer does nothing to feign, simulate' (*ibid*) or impersonate. Many dance pieces would fit into this category. This non-acting is not embedded in 'matrices of pretended or represented character, situation, place, and time' (*ibid* p4). The continuum presented below is a simplification of Kirby's which includes Symbolised and Received acting before Simple Acting (*ibid* p10).

Non-acting Acting

Non-matrixed ------------------ Simple ----------------- Complex
Performing   acting   acting

He explains that 'Acting becomes more complex as more elements are incorporated into the pretence' (p10). So whilst the psychologically and physically transformed character at the height of Neelands' stages may be at the complex acting end of Kirby's continuum, position on the continuum is not determined by issues of style or 'the degree of 'reality', but with what we call, for now, the amount of acting' (*ibid*). Kirby suggests that the same action can be performed in a simple or a complex way and gives an example of someone putting on a jacket. In charades, all that is necessary is to know that the jacket is being put on. However, 'The same action becomes more complex as details such as the resistance of the material, the degree of fit, the weight of the jacket, and so on are acted' (*ibid* p10).

Conceptualising teacher-in-role and the role of teacher

The views presented above make a case for identifying the role of the classroom teacher as a performing role. Although there will be an intention, which Kirby ascribes to theatre as opposed to performance (1987, pxiii), no impersonation or fiction takes place. There is a consciousness of the job in hand and the teacher's relationship to the children. The teacher-in-role is different. Read writes that 'Theatre, by definition, is not this daily domain but an extra-daily dimension, beyond the everyday but ironically dependent upon the everyday realm' (1993, pix). Writers in drama education have sought to identify this extra dimension through a notion of 'significance', as we have seen. Kirby explains the difference by explaining that 'In theatre, the methods and techniques of everyday life are usually altered (1987, pxvi). Earlier in this chapter we saw writers in drama in education describe this altered state with regard to the heightened awareness of aspects such as timing, tension and pace. This clarifies my argument for identifying the teacher-in-role as different from the everyday life activity of teaching.

The following chapters present many attempts to make teacher-in-role a different type of activity from acting, by arguing that acting

is from a script with internal investment and fully rounded characters. They identify acting as one particular genre of acting. However, the continua just examined offer a concept of a broad range
of types of acting. Kirby's description of acting, like Hodge's, is reduced to the impersonation of another:

> If the performer does something to simulate, represent, imper-
> sonate, and so forth, he or she is acting. It does not matter what
> style is used or whether the action is part of a complete charac-
> terisation or informational presentation. No emotion needs to
> be involved. (1996, p46)

Clearly, for performance theorists acting covers a wide range of
types of pretence, some requiring characterisation and some not.
Kirby answers his own question, 'Where are the simplest characteristics of acting?' (1987, p4) by explaining that 'Acting is said to
exist in the smallest and simplest action that involves pretence' (*ibid*
p6-7). With these modes of categorisation, it is hard to argue that
teacher-in-role is not acting. The case studies in chapters 9 and 10
demonstrate that there is equally a range of types of teacher-in-
role, but all would be identified as acting, in Kirby's terms, since
even the minimalist role involves pretence.

Finally, it is worth noting that Kirby promotes a formalist approach
to analysing theatre and performance because the 'content approach is helpless to deal with and therefore rejects' performance
with little or no meaning (1987, px). He sees dealing with the form,
rather than content, as eliminating judgmental effects. He is keen
to produce a model that can be applied equally to the full range of
performance practices. Drama in education practice to date, however, has concerned itself with meaning making. This is due primarily to the pedagogic concern constituent to the practice, at least
when teacher-in-role is employed. While interested in form, it has
been its relationship with the content that has concerned the field.
It is for this reason that, while Kirby chooses a 'nonsemiotic or even
antisemiotic' (*ibid* px) model appropriate to all types of performance, I adopt a semiotic approach in my analysis of the case study
practice, which concerns itself with meaning and content. This also
suits the actor's work in the plot driven play of the third case study.

3
CONTEXTS AND AUDIENCE RELATIONSHIPS

The teacher-in-role and actor are operating in different contexts. The different contexts inevitably affect their relationships with the 'audience'. Given that contexts and audience relationships must influence what the teacher-in-role and actor do, it may seem to follow that they cannot possibly be doing the same thing. The First Model (Table 1) set out in chapter 1, Categorising Teacher-in-role and Actor, identifies many distinctions between the contexts and audience relationships which characterise the teacher-in-role and actor respectively. Let us look at these more closely to see if some of these distinctions can be broken down so that the gap between the two is reduced.

The teacher-in-role is working in an educational institution. The teacher is there to teach the children in her charge. The children cannot get up and walk away without a reaction from the teacher. The teacher must not only focus on adopting a teacher-in-role but must also continue to perform her role as a teacher, since she is responsible for the class. The children are there not voluntarily but compulsorily. This has an effect on the relationship between the teacher-in-role and the audience. The teacher cannot choose to break the expectations of the audience in a major sense. Each teacher is guided by the profession's traditions of practice. Sets of expectations are passed on and the teacher socialised into them.

The choices she has are limited by strong parameters. The children have an expectation that the teacher will teach them – that is the contract between them. Whether or not the children wish to keep their part of the contract, the teacher is obliged to keep hers. The context of the teacher-in-role is the classroom, which for many children has associations of boredom. The teacher-in-role, then, often has to work against negative expectations. The children did not choose the content of the lesson, but must sit through the lesson. The relationship between the content and the audience creates a different context, too. The children in class drama usually know one another. There is a hierarchy between the teacher and the children and an assumed process of knowledge or skills for acquiring it being imparted from the teacher to the children.

The actor is in a theatre. She is not responsible for the members of the audience in the way that the teacher is. The actor can focus fully on the performance with no supervisory concerns. The audience has a very different contract with the performer. Attendance is not compulsory. Audience members have volunteered to attend and have indeed paid to do so. This places an economic contract between the actor and audience. The actor does not need to teach the audience, but the audience must not be bored. If they are bored they will leave and pass on negative comments about the play. If this happens the play may close early and the work will be over sooner than expected. So economics is crucial to the actor-audience relationship. The actor wishes to be admired and to establish a good media image. This will promote her chances of securing high status future contracts. Audience members will have made a choice about the play or the actors in it, and there is an expectation that they will enjoy it. There is an assumption that the actor will give pleasure, but both sides know that the audience has the power to discomfort the actors if it so chooses. Ultimately, the actor's fate is in the hands of the audience, although public dissatisfaction is rarely demonstrated live from an audience in theatre in the United Kingdom. The audiences, unlike those in the schoolroom, do not know each other and often numbers are so large that they will not even see, let alone know who they are collectively.

Diverse contexts for teachers-in-role and actors?

Like the teachers' grid distinguishing teacher-in-role and acting, the differences above suppose that the context for all teachers-in-role is the same and that this is likewise true for actors. But this is not the full picture. I have observed David Booth teaching young children in an infant classroom, a very different context from Fiona Shaw's performance in a West End theatre – but it was also very different from Cecily O'Neill's session in a Royal National Theatre rehearsal room with a teenaged youth theatre. And an actor employed in street theatre in Blackpool has a different context again from Fiona Shaw's. Each individual's context is different and determines audience relationships. Booth needed to maintain the role of 'teacher' with young children whereas O'Neill could approach the youth theatre differently because the participants were there out of choice and were older. The street theatre performer must attract the attention of a possible audience of passersby, while Shaw's audience have committed to give her attention by buying a ticket for the play.

The features above which appear to distinguish the teacher-in-role and the actor not only assume one type of activity for each, but also assume that actors always work within the dominant traditional Western theatre model. Comparisons with many other acting contexts point to less sharp distinctions. The strict boundaries delineated above become a little less solid when we see that two clearly separate modes of teacher-in-role and of acting context and audience relationship do not exist. Here are some examples which break the strict oppositional formula of the grid set out earlier.

When *Waiting for Godot* was performed in a prison, the audience could leave the performance space, but a different context was created because they were incarcerated in the prison (Esslin, 1974, p19). Here the actor's audience was not forced to be at the performance, but their being compulsorily at the prison was significant to the theatrical event. Other theatre events in prisons also challenge a simplistic view of the actor's work. Actors work in prisons with small groups who, unlike audiences in mainstream theatres, might know each other.

Boal's forum theatre also challenges the easy divisions of the grid. The actor in Boal's theatre will work in quite a different context from that assumed by our initial grid distinguishing the actor and teacher-in-role.

	Boal's forum theatre actor	Assumed context of actor (see initial grid)
Audience role	active participation	inactive participation
Audience relationships	familiar	unfamiliar
Audience size	small group	large group

In both traditional Western theatre and contemporary Boalian forum theatre workshops, there is an economic relationship between actor and audience. But this is not the case for all actors. Some provide the audience with free theatre, such as our actor in street theatre for holidaymakers in Blackpool. Here the actor may be paid not from profits from an audience but by a body detached from the theatre experience, such as the council or tourist board. Hard and fast rules about the contexts and relationships with audiences cannot be made. There are so many different forms of theatre that disrupt neat definitions and therefore destabilise simple conclusions that clearly contrast teacher-in-role and acting.

Concepts of audience

I use the word 'audience' generally, to include theatre audiences and children in the classroom. This goes against the published views of writers such as Morgan and Saxton, who declare that 'The teacher must remember that the class is not her audience' (Morgan and Saxton, 1989, p49). They emphasise that the teacher should not focus on her own performance but on the learning potential. But at the heart of their concern is the assumption that an audience is, by definition, non-participant. They mean that the teacher should not be busy in front of the class, with the children just watching. Once the concept of an actively participating audience is conceptualised, calling the children 'audience' is less problematic.

Gavin Bolton's more recent publication, *Acting in Classroom Drama* (1998) draws a comparison between Grotowski's desire for 'audience participation' and what Heathcote wants from children. Grotowski had tried to secure the direct participation of spectators and had put pressure on them to join in with the actors. Grotowski later reflected that this had failed because the audience had arrived unprepared to participate, whereas the actors had the advantage of foreknowledge. Bolton argues that

> The comparison with Grotowski cannot be sustained, of course, when it is realised that Heathcote selected her cards according to her reading of the needs of the class and with a view to giving the pupils the confidence to play their own cards. Grotowski's actors compelled the spectators to join in the actors' play'. (1998, p183)

Heathcote's approach is to take the participants into the drama gradually, while Grotowski's was to exert pressure. Heathcote seems to have a similar aim to John Cage: 'I try to get it so that people realise that they themselves are doing their experience and that it's not being done to them' (cited in *Happenings and Other Acts* edited by M.R. Sandford, 1995, p52). At the same time, Heathcote responded to her perception of the needs of her participating audience. In contrast to Morgan and Saxton's caution about the children not being an audience, Bolton assumes that they are a 'participating audience'. Between the two publications there has been an important shift in the conceptualisations of children's role that is significant to a consideration of teacher/actor relationships with audience.

Concepts of audience in drama in education

I pause to consider this shift from a concept of children being other than an audience to a concept of children being a participatory audience and propose that there was an intermediate step between the two.

Drama in education has continually had to struggle for status at both school and statutory level. Its exclusion from the UK National Curriculum exemplified this. Part of drama's difficulty in gaining recognition was the fact that it was a new subject in terms of both curriculum time and public examinations. A new subject on the curriculum has always had low status. Theatre Studies Advanced level was not accepted by universities as an Advanced level that counted for Higher Education entry when I first started teaching in the mid 1980s. How drama could nonetheless assert its status was an important question. Drama practitioners wanted drama to be taken seriously. The subject had to be legitimised. It deserved a properly recognised place in children's education.

A small group of drama teachers influenced by David Hornbrook felt the way forward was to change the practice of drama in schools, arguing that 'The audience, so neglected by drama-in-education, is fundamental to dramatic art' (Hornbrook, 1998, p110) and that there should be a greater emphasis on formal production. But the majority remained committed to their practice and unwilling to change it. They were, however, prepared to change the discourse when a conceptual shift was presented: to align drama in education with theatre (while maintaining contemporary practice) could be a possible way forward for the status of drama. If seen as a theatre form, it might gain respectability and therefore access to more time in the school day. I suggest that in order to prove that drama in education is a theatre form it was necessary to identify in its practice the features that constitute or define theatre. One of these constituents, it is often argued, is an audience. An audience was seen to categorise theatre, so from a position of audience as irrelevant to classroom drama (Morgan and Saxton, 1989, p49), there was a move to conceptualise participants in drama in education as an audience to their own dramatic action (Neelands, 1990, Introduction). The children could be perceived as an audience for each other while taking part in the drama, drifting in and out of the action and critiquing it in their minds. There was a new articulation of the activity of classroom drama, therefore, introducing theatrical terms to practice that had previously been purged of any theatrical connection. The use of theatre terms has continued and has arguably been a positive move for drama in education's status, particularly perhaps in the eyes of its own body of practitioners.

What is interesting for our purposes is what this move says about perceptions of audience and theatre. Evidently, it embraces a view that an observing audience is a requirement of theatre. While the conceptualisation of drama in education as a theatre form represents a radical contrast with previous conceptualisations of drama in education, it initially tended to operate with a restricted view of theatre. The drive to identify an audience was an attempt to connect drama in education with the western dominant theatre form in which an audience observes action. The logic of this move is understandable if, as I suggest, it was energised by a need for status – for the subject to be legitimised. A new subject seeing itself on the fringe would not wish to identify itself with other practices on the fringe. It needed to be identified with whatever would bring prestige and a degree of power. Interestingly, the form of theatre chosen as the paradigm of theatre was one which in other contexts has been lampooned as bourgeois by some of the theorists and practitioners. This paradox illustrates Foucault's view that it is almost impossible to get away from the discourse in which we are involved, and therefore inevitable that we draw upon that of which we may not approve (1989). What is notable in this context is that drama in education did not claim its credentials by aligning itself to participatory theatre practices which at face value seem more suitable for comparison. Interestingly, when another new theatre form seeks to explain and establish itself, it does not need to prove its credentials as theatre. It is the field peopled by those who are teachers first and artists second that needs to justify its art. Interactive theatre explained here by someone who has trained actors is an example of a collaborative form that does not even consider the need to justify itself, yet it describes practice which is not dissimilar to much drama in education.

> The interactive stage is an environment that encloses both audience, or 'guest', and actor alike. Each guest is, initially or as a matter of course, singularly or as a group, endowed with a role to play. The outcome of any scene may change completely depending upon the actions or response of the guest. These actions or responses continually alter the unfolding drama. The guest, as co-creator, is as responsible for the outcome as the actor. (Izzo, G, (1998) *acting interactive theatre: a handbook,* preface)

The terminology is interesting. The term 'guest' rather than participant (member of audience) may be seen as a way of making the practice look new and unique. Regardless of the semantics, the practice provides yet another example of an actor's context which breaks the mould established in our grid.

It is evident that the simple and taken for granted contrasts between the contexts of the teacher-in-role and actor have been overblown. It is only through delineating theatre to a particular form of western theatre that such contrasts have any plausibility at all. Once other theatre forms are explored the contrasting contexts become much less clear-cut.

4

FUNCTIONS AND AIMS

It is helpful to explain my use of the terms 'functions' and 'aims' and challenge the use of the term function in the discourse of drama in education. References to the concept of the function of teacher-in-role have been used to distance the practice from acting. I draw comparisons between the articulated functions and aims of teacher-in-role and of the actor and I identify the neglected parallels between the functions of teacher roles and the functions of theatrical roles.

Functions and aims are inter-related but their relationship requires clarifying. An aim is defined as seeking 'to attain or achieve ... a purpose, a design, an object aimed at' (Oxford English Dictionary, 1990, p24). A function is defined as 'a mode of action or activity by which a thing fulfils its purpose' (*ibid*, p477). The aim for the teacher-in-role is that which is to be achieved, such as a new insight into a familiar fairy story. The function of the teacher-in-role is the mode of action that will fulfil her aim. The teacher-in-role's purpose in this example would be to bring about a new insight into a familiar fairy story. The aim of the teacher-in-role is to achieve particular learning objectives; the function of the teacher-in-role is to do what must be done to ensure that these are achieved. The aim, then, is the ends, and the function is the means to achieve those ends.

The literature of drama in education contains much about the function of the teacher-in-role and focuses upon enabling learning, and its pedagogic efficiency, 'to maximise the learning possibilities' (Kitson and Spiby, 1997, p38). The function is frequently used to distinguish teacher-in-role from acting. Cecily O'Neill argues, for example, that 'Teachers in role must never act in the sense that an actor may, because they have a different job to do, a separate function' (O'Neill, 1995a, p61) and that teacher-in-role 'is defined by its function' (*ibid* p78).

A challenge to functionalism

The comfortable use of the word function in the discourse of drama in education should no longer go unchallenged. The term function asserts a scientific, almost automatic inevitability. The heart's function is to beat, to pump blood around the body. The heart cannot function as anything else. It exists to fulfil its function of pumping blood. In this scientific model the word function takes on a non-negotiable meaning. The heart's function could not be argued to be anything other than to pump blood around the body. There is consensus about what the heart's function is. There is, however, no such consensus about what the teacher-in-role does or indeed should be doing. The term function, therefore may be masquerading as a consensus, where in fact there is none.

Within sociology, an analogy between social organism and the biological organism promoted a particular theoretical approach: functionalism. Durkheim, in providing the framework for a functionalist perspective of education, established a view that for society to operate effectively individuals must develop a sense of belonging to something wider than their immediate situation (Durkheim, 1964 [1895]). Education in this view provides the mechanism by which society's norms and values are transmitted to children. Functionalists therefore see education as a crucial part of the socialisation process. What functionalists fail to take into account, however, is that there may be more than one set of values in society. A high level of consensus cannot actually be assumed. With its concentration on social order and value consensus, functionalism largely ignores the existence of coercion and conflict in society. What is more, if the education system does transmit values, they may well be those of the ruling class or elite. It is arguably the case, therefore, that identifying something as a function camouflages a value judgement.

There is in fact no consensus about the function of theatre and acting, as we shall see. Asked about the function of an actor, David Mamet might talk of delivering the lines written by the playwright. Asked the same question, Joan Littlewood might have talked of the responsibility of devising, of personal input and experience. To argue that the function of acting is such and such does imply what is inevitable and unchangeable. In fact, the views would have been articulated from different standpoints, and neither can claim an absolute authority. Equally, to say that education or working as teacher-in-role have functions assumes a particular consensual value system that asserts what the function should be. So a description of what does take place is seen as a description of what it is thought should take place. Veiled behind an assumed consensus is a value-laden assertion.

As a result of the challenges we have seen which expose functionalism as controlling and value-laden, notions of function have been purged from most education discourses. However, it has remained in the discourse of drama in education. There is frequent reference to the function of teacher-in-role in the literature, and the assertion that it has a different function from that of the actor. The function of teacher-in-role appears to be basically to deliver the pedagogic purpose. In the light of what we know about functionalism, we might wonder whether there is an assumed set of values behind the use of the term. It may be that the term function gives a scientific gloss and thus credence to an assumed consensus.

In the light of this theoretical development, I suggest two points. Firstly, that far from being an independent issue, function, as the term is used in drama in education, is as value laden as the term aims, and is entirely bound up with the aims. Secondly, that there is no consensus among drama practitioners about the function of teacher-in-role.

I have drawn upon dictionary definitions of aim and function that led to a notion of aims as what is sought to be achieved and function as the means by which these aims would be reached. There is no challenge to a view that aims are created given particular value systems. The aims of the school curriculum are partly driven by the value system of the political party in power. An obvious example is the UK Conservative party's edict on Section 28 outlawing any promotion of homosexual relationships in schools. The school management team usually has some influence on the aims of the learning experience of its children. There is also the teacher. Drama teachers openly debate the values behind the aims for their lessons. Whether they are worthy aims, contentious aims, racist aims or liberal aims are discussed. Recent examples include Peter O'Connor's challenge to the aims of Brian Edmiston's lesson on Christopher Columbus (2000). John O'Toole challenges the aims of many dramas for being obsessively politically correct (2001). So we accept that our aims are value-laden and are comfortable discussing them.

However, the word function has been used as though it is innocent of such influences. Yet if a function serves to provide the means to an end, then it is as value laden as the aims because it is delivering the aims. Ultimately then, there is no significant difference between aims and functions as the terms have been used in the discursive formation of drama in education. Both are driven by a specific value system.

My second point is that there is no consensus about the function of teacher-in-role. The use of the word function has assumed that there is a shared understanding of what that function is; a consensus. However, if function is tied to aims as I have suggested, then disputes over the values of aims confirm that there is no fixed, agreed notion of function. Let us examine a particular instance by way of example.

'Three Looms Waiting' was Heathcote's drama famously filmed by the BBC's Omnibus (1970). After the lesson, Heathcote was interviewed about her ideas and her perception of what had taken place. During the lesson the boys had been negotiating the location for their drama. Having established a London location, Heathcote asked where in London. A boy said, 'Coventry'. Heathcote ignored the boy's mistake that Coventry is in London and during the interview she justifies her decision to do so. It was irrelevant to what she, the teacher, wanted to achieve. Her aims had nothing to do with geography. Another teacher in a UK primary school, perhaps during an inspection, may make a different decision if a child had made the same mistake. She may stop the drama to explain, but more likely she would find a way within the drama, in role, to clarify the fact that Coventry is not in London. This teacher could also justify her decision. She knows what she wants to achieve. Presumably, both teachers would articulate the function of teacher-in-role differently. It can be seen to excite and liberate, on the one hand. It can, on the other, be seen as functioning to deliver the requirements of the national curriculum and is therefore bound by an assumption that misinformation should be corrected. It may not be deemed appropriate for a boy to leave the classroom talking about Coventry in London. It may, however, be deemed appropriate if the child had a positive learning experience beyond the geographical detail. In these contexts there is no consensus about what the teacher-in-role should be doing.

At the heart of the process/curriculum debate that Neelands considers (2000) is a lack of consensus about the aims and functions of teacher-in-role. It may not be a huge chasm, but inherent in these positions lie differences in assumptions concerning what drama should be doing and what the function is of the teacher-in-role. Heathcote's Omnibus lesson represents a process bias in which the aims are established through her reading of the needs of the class. The function of the teacher-in-role is to ensure these aims are met. The example of the primary teacher above represents the view of curriculum drama. The aims for her lessons are often those set by the curriculum designers. She may need to ensure that particular spellings or towns or historical events are learnt during the drama. If the aims for teachers are different – and since functions are inextricably bound up with aims – the continued use of the term function may lead to a false assumption of consensus.

Comparisons between teacher and actor functions and aims

When writing about role, drama in educationalists do focus on the function, as explained by Morgan and Saxton: 'The teacher's eye and ear must monitor what is going on, how time is passing and if the educational objectives are being met' (1989, p49).

This is not unique to teachers-in-role. In some contexts actors, too, must monitor what is taking place, time passing and whether objectives are being met. In Theatre in Education (Alcock, 1999) for example, and some forms of Theatre for Development (Kerr, 1995) it is crucial for actors to ensure educational objectives are achieved, and in much traditional African theatre a sense of social instruction is paramount (Okpewho, 1990, Biodun, 1984).

Both teacher-in-role and actor

* have the job of creating a fiction; operate in the 'as if'
* interact with those with whom they share the space
* function as communicators employing external features in order to hint at internal concerns

These are significant similarities. Both create a context that is feigned, and behave as if that context were real. They interact with other participants in, or observing, the fiction on both the level of locus (abstract) platea (concrete) (Counsell, 1996, p163). Both use external features such as gestures and facial expressions to indicate intentions and motives. Despite these important similarities, distinctions have continually been drawn. These are the differences I have identified in the literature. I analyse each in turn to see if a broader concept of theatre makes the differences less significant.

The differences between the functions of teacher-in-role and actor are:

* The actor has a function to entertain, the teacher-in-role to instruct
* The actor functions to elicit applause
* The actor functions to follow a predetermined destiny in the performance
* The teacher-in-role has many functions, the actor just one

The actor has a function to entertain, the teacher-in-role to instruct

Please don't act! The teacher must remember that the class is not her audience. It is not you as performer or entertainer that is important, but the learning which your role can stimulate. (Morgan and Saxton, 1989, p49)

I wish to challenge both points and argue that they cannot operate as clear-cut distinguishing features since teachers-in-role also need to entertain and actors often associate their function with instruction. Getting a balance of entertainment and instruction is crucial in classroom drama as in many forms of theatre.

Geoff Gillham articulated the importance of this balance with his phrase 'play for kids' and 'play for teacher' (Gillham, 1974). The play for kids represents the entertainment aspect and the play for teacher is obviously the instruction. The teacher needs to generate the children's interest in the drama in order to keep them involved. The chance to carry out any teaching will evaporate if the children have lost interest. Theatre, too, must entertain to keep its audience's interest. In many theatre genres there is an intention to instruct, a desire for learning to take place. Theatre in education must educate and entertain. This is nothing new. Horace's *Ars Poetica* argued that theatre should entertain and educate. Brecht's familiar concept of theatre as a vehicle for teaching requires an entertainment function to keep the audience's attention and indeed, presence (1986, [1957] pp69-76). The increasingly popular theatre for health promotion and theatre for development will foreground this balance while planning their performances (Ball, 2001).

An actor functions to elicit applause

This tacit invitation from the actor for approval from an audience is surely only residually part of TIR. (Bolton, email 2001)

Bolton cites expectation of applause as the defining feature of performance (1998, p262). However, even this may be seen as no longer a feature to separate the teacher and actor. Modern installations, often with no specific ending, which continue as audiences move in and out, function as work in progress and therefore no applause is expected. Actors in forum theatre do not invite applause. I recall a GCSE drama group arguing with an assessor about why they had not come back for a curtain call after their performance. They wanted the audience to be left with the message of world poverty and not with them as performers. They said the attention would be drawn to them rather than the charity boxes they had placed in the theatre space.

The teacher-in-role does not wish to attract applause, but it is not unknown to receive it. Bolton 'once had an embarrassing experience ... in which before an audience of teachers [he] addressed them in role thinking that [he] was successfully 'drawing them in' to '*our play*' and they clapped!' (email 2001). Neelands' definition of performing (1998, p9) points out that in the western tradition of theatre there is an assumption that audience is separated from the performers, 'But performance can also mean a dramatic event that is shared among a group'. In these cases there may not be any anticipation of applause. On closer analysis of both teacher-in-role and actor, it becomes hard to maintain the view that a desire for applause will always distinguish the two.

The actor has a predetermined destiny in the performance
In acting one is 'no longer free to shift around spontaneously'. (Morgan and Saxton, 1989, p35)

This point is tied up with a view that the drama in education class does not follow a written script, but the actor's work does. Certainly, an actor playing Hamlet has a teleological function, a particular job to do in order to fulfil the tragedy. Although his destiny is determined to some extent by the script, there will also be a prepared plan according to the overall production decisions. However, the actor does not necessarily have a predetermined destiny in the performance, nor a written script. Improvised theatre (Izzo, 1998) and Boal's invisible theatre (1979) do not provide the actor with a complete destiny. Indeed, Roddy Maude-Roxby of the improvising company, Theatre Machine, writes, 'I think the most important moment in improvisation is when you don't know what will happen next' (cited in Frost and Yarrow, 1990, p55). In Commedia actors know the overall direction of where they are going, but they must respond to the unpredictable comments from the audience and each other. Rudlin sees the plays as 'self authored' (1994, p1). The improvised theatre demands that the actors enter the performance space with mental agility and willingness to respond.

It seems to me that the best and most direct initiation into improvised comedy will be by watching children at play...children who play well, who know how to play, are models of verve, naturalness and invention. They are masters of improvisation. (Copeau, 1990 [1916] p155)

In these examples the actor, just like the teacher-in-role, can vary responses according to the impetus of the moment. The function does not require a prescribed script to be followed, but a creative and immediate response to what is given by fellow actors or audience. It should be added that even in scripted performances, we expect actors to respond to the moment and to change as they develop their ideas about the role. It is said of Brando that 'long after opening night, he continued to explore, adding and changing and removing, adjusting his performance according to how he felt on the spot' (Hirsch, 1984, p297).

The teacher-in-role has many functions, the actor just one

The leader or teacher, working inside the creative process, may acquire some of the functions of the director, designer, stage manager and even audience, but because of the nature of the activity, will go beyond these purposes. The leader's primary tasks are those of managing the action, of operating the structure, and of functioning as a dramatist. (O'Neill, 1995, p64)

I do not wish to challenge the fact that teacher-in-role has many functions, only the implication that this makes it different from the actor. In many performance contexts the actor, too, has various dramatic functions. We look first at the comparisons made with teacher-in-role and then consider the actor's functions.

Neelands recognises the multifaceted nature of teacher-in-role by equating teacher-in-role with Boal's 'joker' (1998, p66). The joker sets up the rules in forum theatre and moves between the audience and the acting, supervising the change of actors and remains not 'tied down to an allegiance to performer' (Schutzman and Cohen-Cruz, 1994, p237). Interestingly, the one thing the joker is not, is an actor. In this comparison, Neelands associates the functions of teacher-in-role taking a role, but also being a teacher with an educational agenda. She must:

– be a listener
– respond to what is offered
– incorporate the ideas of the participants
– keep an eye on the time
– act as director of the drama

– act as a playwright
– participate in the action
– represent a role or roles.

For the most part, however, the comparisons refer to roles in traditional mainstream theatre. The teacher-in-role is frequently aligned to the work of the theatre director (O'Neill, 1995), the playwright (2000) and the dramatist (Bolton, 1998). Bolton suggests that the '...teacher-in-role's function is that of a dramatist' (1998, p184), but a dramatist not outside the action but within it. What is meant by 'dramatist' is explained: 'As dramatist the teacher is dictating at both structural and thematic levels' (*ibid* p184) By the term 'dramatist' Bolton seems to mean the dramaturgical function. The dramatist comparison seems similar to O'Neill's identification of the teacher-in-role with the job of playwright who also 'has an eye to structural and thematic concerns' (2000).

There are clearly good reasons for ascribing the functions of the dramatist, director and playwright as the theatrical equivalents to the functions of the teacher-in-role. They all suggest a sense of 'behind the scenes', the enabling process, the setting up of things to enable the creativity of others. However, these concepts are slippery. The role of the director in contemporary theatre and performance is seen in many different ways. Simon of Theatre de Complicite has a notion of directing that bears little resemblance to that of Sir Richard Eyre (1992). Counsell suggests that 'even the term writer has come under scrutiny as the writer contributes but one part of the total performance 'text'' (1996, p5).

The actor working under a traditional director may have no other function than to perform a part. However, this is not always the case. Chekov's actors are charged with understanding all the constituent aspects of production. Chekov assumed that his actors should, to some degree, be also directors. There are many theatrical examples where an actor may be required to fulfil numerous functions. New models of playwriting involve the actor in a wide range of functions, too. The ensemble methods of Joint Stock (Ritchie, 1987) and the approach of Joan Littlewood are well known examples of shared playwriting (Goorney, 1981). Many contemporary companies devise work themselves as a company, all taking part in the process and in the product, such as Frantic Assembly, DV8, and Peepolikus.

Most interesting, perhaps, is a comparison with the Commedia dell'arte actor.

In Commedia dell'arte, all the company members know the story line, but actors improvise within it, and must respond to whatever the audience give them. My memory of playing Arlecchino, the Harlequin, is of having to think quickly on my feet because the audience heckled throughout. In my comments to the audience, I had to bear in mind what had happened before, the other characters, and of course the general drift of the story line towards which we were all working. Tension was still required, secrets could not be given away, hints of agendas had to be given but we could add no additional story lines that could not be fulfilled within the performance.

Features from the Teacher-In-Role functions list	Reasons why the functions are relevant to the Commedia actor
Be a listener	to hear audience's contributions
Respond to what is offered	to create the live exchange of the genre
Incorporate the ideas of the participants	to highten the improvisation experience
Keep an eye on the time	since to spend too long at one time may have consequences for later in the performance
Act as director of the drama	orchestrate scenarios in the moment
Act as a playwright	since no complete script exists
Participate in the action	as a company member
Representing a role	As one of the familiar commedia characters

If we return to the functions of the teacher-in-role listed earlier, we find that each represent a dramaturgical function of the Commedia actor. The table charts each feature from the list, alongside the reason that it is equally important to the actor.

These lists illustrate the ways that both teacher-in-role and the commedia actor perform many identical functions at the same time. Each function ascribed to the teacher-in-role is also present for the commedia actor. There is very much a sense of Johnstone's (1999) 'playing in the moment' in both dramatic forms. Rather than the mutifunctional aspect of teacher-in-role distinguishing it from the actor, in the light of many theatrical contexts, it brings it closer.

Concepts of shared playwriting are closer to what the teacher-in-role is doing in the classroom context. Teachers share the process with the children and ultimately aim to minimize the power differentials between class and teacher; 'by working in role we, as teachers, are able to establish a pattern of relationships which enable negotiation, joint ownership and the sharing of power even if elsewhere the normative role of the teacher is a traditional one' (Carey, 1990). These processes engage the whole group rather than one individual, and thus it is difficult to pin the function of director and playwright entirely on the teacher-in-role. There is a shared ideology that ties teachers of drama in education and collaborative theatre workers such as Joan Littlewood. Both are working in a deliberately democratised way. Both wish to share the creative processes and to give voice to participants. Both accept experiment as part of the theatrical journey and engage participants in that journey. The activity is led by a sense of the value of personal discovery and group articulation of those discoveries. Littlewood drew on popular art forms to create performance, so that singing and dancing were incorporated. She knew her audience in London's East End would be familiar with the old time music hall tradition, so it was exploited in performance. Similarly, drama teachers frequently draw on popular art forms, most commonly perhaps from television programmes including soap operas and documentaries.

Commedia dell'arte is not the only dramatic context in which an actor plays many roles. Direct connections between the teacher and actor's creation of the plot function can be identified. The teacher-in-role has a skeleton plot framework in her mind. The flesh on the bones are the business of the participants. The analogy of a journey is often used to explain this approach. 'If the drama lesson is conceived as a map, with a series of reference points and alternative routes, the structure becomes more flexible and allows the children to make the choices that we've been talking about...We could see on the map where we wanted to get to, and it didn't matter how many diversions we had to take' (Kitson and Spiby, 1995, p41). The route taken is altered according to the decisions the participants make, but the teacher ensures that somehow the destination is reached by the end so pedagogic intentions are fulfilled. (There are some variations on the degree to which the teacher should adhere to particular aims rather than move with the interests of the class. Process versus curriculum variations though touched upon earlier regarding Three Looms Waiting and the location of Coventry, are not the focus for this thesis.) The notion of a journey may seem rather Aristotelian in its plot dominance, but the journey may take turns and loops, so that there is opportunity for re-examination and investigation rather than just a delivery of plot line. 'Who dunnit?' murder weekends operate in a similar fashion. The company has prepared certain moments that the participants will experience. These are the A to Bs of this theatre form. What takes place between the planned moments can vary according to what the participants offer. The actors need to keep the next stop (B or C) in their minds and guide the action accordingly. This echoes commedia practice described above.

Actors in Littlewood's theatre, in McBurney's or in Murder Mysteries can be described as dramatists or playwrights creating oral texts to keep the overall piece on track. Comparisons with such work have not been made in the literature on drama in education due to the dominant assumption that actors work from written or literary texts. In fact, many theatre forms work with an oral text as the examples demonstrate. This reasserts the point that weight has been given to the literary aesthetic in the literature of drama in education, at the expense of the oral aesthetic which I suggest is far closer to the practice of drama in education. In such devised texts, actors have many functions, just as do teachers-in-role.

The functions of the roles

In the theatre, if you ask an actor what role he is playing, he is more likely to answer with the name, rather than the function, of the character ('Henry V' rather than the one in charge). In educational drama, what is important is the function of the role in both the dramatic interaction and in stimulating learning. (Morgan and Saxton, 1987, pp41-42)

Here a distinction is drawn. Many writers have considered the functions of teacher roles (Clipson-Boyles, 1998, Morgan and Saxton, 1987), but what has not yet been considered is the function of the roles in relation to the extensive literature on the functions of theatrical roles. O'Neill provides a commentary on the functions of character in theatrical contexts, pointing out that 'characterisation depends on function' (1995, p71), but does not relate these to the functions of the teacher-in-role's role or character. Writers have taken the view that a teacher-in-role's role cannot be a character since it has a function. It is arguable, however, that all characters have functions. They serve the logic of the plot, the spirit of the mood or the play's theme. The character versus plot argument arising from Aristotle's poetics has continued through the ages (Halliwell (ed), 1987). But whichever view is taken, the function of character is accepted. William Archer (1912, p218) highlights the issue explaining that the character can appear to come first given that Romeo and Juliet's tragedy would not have occurred had Romeo not been the impetuous young man he was shown to be early in the play. In this example, the character functions to form the plot. Conversely, it could be argued that he was depicted as impetuous, since this would function to serve the plot's tragedy. Whether plot leads character or character leads plot, the character still serves a function.

The theories of Vladimir Propp define the common contemporary view of character as function since characters fulfil the plot. 'In respect of the application of semiotic methodology to character, an important legacy from the early structuralist and formalist approaches has been the concept of the functions of character. Most famous for beginning the work in this area is the formalist, Propp, who identified thirty-one functions of the fairy tale. He explained that 'many functions logically join together into certain spheres.

These spheres *in toto* correspond to their respective performers. They are spheres of action (1968, p79). Propp identified seven characters that either 'correspond exactly to the action, or a character changes its function through being involved in several spheres of action, or one sphere of action is carried out by several characters' (Aston and Savona, 1991, p36).

1. Villain

2. Donor (provider)

3. Helper

4. Princess (a sought after person) and her father

5. Dispatcher

6. Hero

7. False hero

Propp had studied Russian folktales and forged the way for structuralists, such as Ubersfeld (1978) to identify functions within performance texts. The functions of characters in the performance texts of the drama class can be identified similarly. Drama in education can be deconstructed in the same way as we might deconstruct a play in order to discover how the roles have functioned in their development. Later I seek to identify the role functions of the roles taken when I analyse the case studies.

Aston and Savona identify the function of character as governed by convention.

> Given that plot, in Greek tragic drama, is constituted through the reordering of material received in the form of mythic narrative, it is apparent that character has attracted to itself a narrative function from the beginning of theatre, and that a repertoire of conventionalised operations governing the communication of information to the spectator has developed over time. (1991, p44)

They then provide a list of eight of the main conventions they have identified in which the character delivers narrative to the spectators. I draw attention to two. The first: 'Self-presentation. A character may introduce herself/himself at the start of the play, as does Oedipus in *Oedipus the King* (1958), and/or offer supplementary information as appropriate in the course of the action' (Aston and Savona, 1991, p44). This parallels the way many teacher roles function in class drama. Both O'Neill's and O'Toole's opening roles in the case studies function precisely in this way. A teacher role introduces herself and provides necessary information for the imminent action. The fourth convention is 'Character as confidant(e). A further conventional method of communicating information is the provision of a minor character in whom a more important character may confide' (Aston and Savona, 1991, p44). This describes the familiar teacher-in-role go-between roles who have access to information from someone more powerful, but their lack of power makes them accessible to the other characters/ participants. The field of drama in education too, has produced lists to describe the possibilities for these go-between roles. The role can function as an information giver, or an information seeker, a high or low status role, an intermediary or 'one of the gang' (Morgan and Saxton, 1987, p40-49, Kitson and Spiby, 1997, p56).

Aston and Savona conclude that the actor is in role for two reasons: to communicate a character, and to serve a function – which could be pedagogic. Here, then, character and function are not set up as oppositions.

Examining functions and role functions has proved complex. It has led to a concern that *function* has been used to masquerade as innocent, while in fact, it cannot be separated from an overall aim which by its nature, will be value-laden. Furthermore, it has revealed that it is not possible to distinguish teacher-in-role from acting through notions of function. Indeed, we discover that the functions of the teacher-in-role are very similar to those of many actors.

5

SKILLS REQUIRED FOR TEACHER-IN-ROLE AND ACTING

The extensive literature on the aims and functions of teacher-in-role has not been matched by work on the skills required to fulfil them. When it is argued that the teacher-in-role functions as dramatist, for example, we assume certain skills are implied. But while a general explanation about shaping the dramatic experience is offered, the skills involved in the process of creating teacher role have not been covered in the writing. Bolton has recently pointed out that 'no one appears to have gone thoroughly into teacher-in-role. Most of us have talked about its 'functions' but rarely go into its component skills' (email 2001).

What are the skills for teacher-in-role?

O'Neill has created a list entitled, 'Teachers in process drama should see themselves as...' The list includes 'artists, the teachers collaborating with their students, the co-artists' (O'Neill, 1995 p13). This gives a sense of a creative process, but does not identify specific skills. Margaret Burke (1995), constructing thirteen basic principles for the training of a drama teacher, lists some significant skills that are specific to the drama teacher. Skill 3, for example, is important to the drama process: 'Teachers must acquire the analytical skills which enable them to sift through what students are saying to generate dramatic action' (p42), and Skill 5 'Teachers must have the knowledge of enough strategies in order to be able to frame their choice of activity effectively – and affectively' (p42). However, none of the thirteen skills make reference to acting, use of voice, or gesturing. Burke speaks of the art of 'making significant' as what 'causes that which is set apart to resonate meaning beyond itself, beyond the obvious' (Burke, 1995 p44), but not about how the articulation of a role is significant in achieving this. Nor is there any suggestion of the skills required to take a role. Neelands considers the roles, skills and knowledge of the drama teacher in *Beginning Drama* (1998). Key skills are identified as questioning, contracting and structuring. Advice is given for using teacher-in-role: 'Use teacher-in-role to initiate, model, guide and control the students' responses; build atmosphere; work as a storyteller within the story' (1998, p66). But all these points could apply to the teacher in her usual teaching context except the fact that the storyteller works 'within' the story.

Arguably, the most significant article on drama and theatre in education practice is Dorothy Heathcote's 'Sign (and portents?)' (1982, pp18-28). In it she describes the strengths of the theatre in education actor and then explains that 'a teacher by her inability to strongly sign on clothing, setting and accuracy of properties, can sign mainly in the language and body position areas, and these are more easily shed than the clothing and prop signs of the TiE actor' (*ibid*). This implies that the teacher-in-role is using the skills of the actor, but without the many extras the theatre in education actor can employ. The signing is significant for both. This can be seen to imply that the teacher is acting, but without such a strong ability to 'sign strongly' in certain respects. This is reminiscent of Kirby's non-acting/acting continuum. 'The simplest acting is that in which only one element or dimension of acting is used' (1987, p10). It is conceived not as something other than acting but as 'simple acting.

Signalling the attitudes and intentions of the role clearly is the most important thing a drama teacher does when she is working in role ... Voice, language, gesture and bearing which are appropriate to the drama, the role and the learning, must be carefully chosen and maintained. (Morgan and Saxton, 1987, p62)

The skills to use 'voice, language, gesture and bearing' are necessary for the teacher using role. Also necessary, therefore, is an understanding of which gestures are required at which precise moment. As in theatre, the 'process of signification is directed and controlled' (Aston and Savona, 1991, p99) so that the children are able to interpret what they see and hear. Bolton explores the notion of children 'reading' what is provided for them by the teacher-in-role. He provides an example of a lesson in which Heathcote played a few different roles to which the children responded differently. They were responding to what they 'read' in her roles and she responded in turn to what she read in their responses. Bolton refers to the teacher's function as 'a dramatist who not only is supplying the words but also the accompanying non-verbal signals, so that the 'reading' required of the pupils is multi-dimensional' (Bolton, 1998, p184).

'The concept of 'reading' the actor has its origins in theatre semiotics' (Watson, 1995), so by 'multidimensional', Bolton is referring to the systems which communicate meaning beyond the spoken word. Certainly Glyn Wickham has repeatedly claimed that only 40 per cent of the communication of theatre is through the dialogue, and 60 per cent is through the other aspects of the signing system such as voice, gesture, space, lighting and set (Wickham, 1967). The teacher may not have so many aspects of communication available, as we have seen, but this does not imply a distinction between teacher-in-role and actor.

It is clear from Bolton's description that the teacher needs to be aware of how non-verbal signals are used. These non-verbal signing skills are not distinct to teachers. This is what Styan says *a propos* acting:

> Dramatic meaning cannot lie in words alone, but in voices and the tone of voices, in the pace of speaking and the silences between the gesture and expression of the actor, physical distinctions between him and others. (Styan, 1975, p26)

Bolton explains that children in Heathcote's classes are asked to look for implications, motivations and assess consequences. The way they identify implications, motivations and assess consequences is by noting the way she looks at them, her tone of voice and her gestures. As Bolton has pointed out, and Styan above, they look beyond the words.

> The most common case of the subject in the drama is the 'figure of the actor'. The figure of the actor is the dynamic unity of an entire set of signs, the carrier of which may be the actor's body, voice, movements... (Veltrusky, 1964, p84)

The audience decodes. It interprets what is encoded through the actor (Watson, 1995). To understand both the teacher-in-role and the actor the child participants or audience are expected to decode the figure of the actor. But even though we have seen that this is a process undergone between the teacher and children, as between the actor and audience, there remains a persistent reluctance to equate teacher-in-role with acting. When Bowell and Heap explain that the teacher does not need to be a good actor because 'teacher-in-role is not about acting in the external sense of putting on a costume and finding a voice and a set of mannerisms for a character' the implication is, of course, that acting is. The skills required are different, we are told, because the teacher role is 'concerned with enabling the children to enter the drama' (2001, p47). Although assumed voice and mannerisms are not required for role, writers suggest that teachers need not be afraid of role since they are giving 'performances' in the classroom anyway as teachers. As teachers 'we modify the way we speak, our facial expressions and body language, we deliver 'our dialogue' ... we often withhold what we know, in order to create an effect. Under these circumstances we are playing the part of a teacher – we are acting the role' (p47).

This is fascinating in that it suggests that there is more acting behaviour involved in being a teacher in the classroom than there is in being a teacher-in-role, as discussed in chapter 2. We change our voice and gesture as teachers in normal classroom practice, but we do not need to do so when we take a role in the dramatic fiction. This emphasises how the notion of acting in role really is taboo. The skills required for the role of teacher, then, are those which can produce altered behaviour. The skills for role are those required to enable children to enter the drama, but they do *not* require costume, voice or mannerism changes. The fact is that actors are not always required to use costume and change their voices and adopt special mannerisms. Indeed, Grotowski sought a theatre that was stripped of costume, make-up and everything beyond the actor/ audience relationship. He describes the exciting discovery that theatre could exist without all these things; it was the actor audience relationship that was crucial (1968, p12). It is thus the skills in developing this relationship that are significant to the actor. The same could be said of the teacher-in-role.

Chris Lawrence describes using 'the vocabulary of drama – such as gesture, eye contact, use of symbols and space' in a role he took during a lesson taught by Heathcote (Lawrence, 1982, p4). He wore a costume for Albert the tramp, and explains the choice of articles of clothing in the same way as a costume designer would for an actor's costume. It operated at a symbolic, as well as literal level. The connection is not made between the actor and teacher-in-role, but the costuming reminds us of the overlap. Ian Spiby makes a direct, explicit connection between the actor and the teacher-in-role. It may not be coincidence that Spiby has spent more of his career in drama than in drama in education. His writing is striking for its theatrical connections, being significantly different from that even of his co writer in *Drama 7-11* (1997). Under the heading of 'Signing the role' he explains that when taking a teacher role, 'one of the most important points to consider is signing ... we give clues about the role we are presenting' (p58). He makes a comparison with signals we give in everyday life through 'what we wear, what we say, how we move, what we do, the tone of our voice, the words that we speak' (p59).

So far, this is similar to what Bolton, Morgan and Saxton and Brian Heap have said, but Spiby goes on to point out that 'Actors with many years' experience will use all of these signals to convey the role that they are playing. As a teacher it would be difficult to emulate this fully but what we are able to do is utilise some of these skills to improve our in-role characterisation' (p59). Here, as in Heathcote's 'Signs (and portents?)', what a teacher does in role is associated with what an actor does in role. It also explicitly argues that teacher-in-role requires some skills which are the actor's skills. Spiby does imply that the full range of skills of the actor would be an advantage, but just minimal acting skills or a single skill could still be used effectively. A significant skill, therefore, may be the selection of what could support the drama, such as a particular voice, a prop or item of costume, as well as the skills in carrying them off in role.

Even here, however, where the skills of the actor are shown as desirable for the teacher-in-role, the teacher-in-role is not explicitly described as acting. What emerges from surveying the literature is that although it is not described as 'acting', the teacher-in-role, like the actor, is signing. In most cases, though, the signing system is compared to that which we use in everyday life, rather than the sign system of theatre, as was identified in Chapter 2.

What are the skills for actor training?

Seeking a similar profile of what are seen to be the skills necessary for acting in professional theatre, I turned to the National Council for Drama Training's document, *Criteria and Procedures for Accreditation of Courses* (November, 1999). It provides 'criteria, listing technical skills and creative abilities' that visiting panel will use in making a judgement about a course' (7.3). Courses are assessed in the 'core skills of Acting, Voice and Movement' (7.31). It is interesting that voice and movement are separated from acting, since use of voice and movement will be part of what enables a student to achieve the acting criteria, such as 'show evidence of the skills of characterisation'. The document does not explain the skills of characterisation, but these criteria have been drawn up to facilitate assessment rather than facilitate enquiry into the nature of performance. However, this list which accreditation panels will use to 'look for evidence that student actors are being offered learning experiences appropriate to their years of study' (7.33) enabling them to achieve particular core skills in acting is of interest to me because it lists what the council believes to be 'core skills of Acting' (7.32). Here are the core skills then. Let's take them one by one to see if there are any parallels between the skills of the actor and the teacher-in-role.

7.33 ACTING: In assessing the quality of work in Acting, Accreditation Panels and Monitors will look for evidence that student actors are being offered learning experiences, appropriate to their year of study, which will enable them to:

a) *develop and play a character in rehearsals and performances and sustain it before an audience within the framework of a production as directed*

The teacher requires these skills to maintain a role within the framework of the dramatic encounter. In a processual developing model, each lesson may be seen as a role rehearsed for the next time the drama is taught.

b) *show evidence of the skills of characterisation*

Drama books are full of teacher roles that reveal character, be it the mischievous Jack or the greedy giant, and O'Toole's roles reveal characterisation skills – as we shall see in chapter 10.

c) *create believable character and emotion appropriate to the demands of the text and production*

If the children did not believe in the character of Suzie and her fear of the snow, the drama could not proceed (Ackroyd, 1994).

d) *define the objectives of a character and embody and express these within the context of a production*

Teachers define the objectives of their roles as 'functions', as we saw in chapter 4.

e) *make full use of individuality of performance*

Skills of individuality of performance may not be required in teacher-in-role.

f) *work sensitively with other actors in rehearsal and performance*

Such skills are required for the teacher-in-role to work with the participants.

g) *show evidence within performance of creative imagination, emotion, thought, concentration and energy*

Teachers-in-role require skills of concentration and energy, but are not required to 'show' them.

h) *develop an effective working process and the ability to monitor and evaluate its application*

Monitoring and evaluation of the working process are crucial to teacher-in-role.

i) *draw upon and make use of personal experience and observation to assist in the creation of role*

This may be an inevitability rather than a skill, since teacher roles are created from what we know from life, stories we have read, and from previous drama experience.

j) prepare and sustain the quality of concentration necessary for each performance
A key skill for teacher-in-role.

k) combine acting with singing and/or dancing and other appropriate skills within a performance
Probably not a required skill.

l) use make-up, costumes and props effectively to develop performance
Skills with props are useful. This might involve the way they are handled to give particular significance to them (Ackroyd, 1998; Lawrence, 1982; Kitson and Spiby, 1997)

m) communicate to an audience with expression, emotion and spontaneity
Skills of spontaneity are essential.

n) adjust to the demands of different venues and media
Teachers employ skills enabling them to adjust to the different physical environments in which they teach, such as dinner halls, open plan areas and the table filled classrooms. Similarly, they adapt their work according to the technical facilities available.

o) adjust to the nature and reaction of different audiences
Essential skills for teacher-in-role.

p) read and interpret texts, research and observation in the development of a role
Certainly teacher roles often need research, but the research usually focuses upon the subject matter rather than a particular role. Many teachers do take roles of particular characters which would need specific research, such as Morgan and Saxton's example of Claudius speaking to the court about Hamlet (1987, p64).

q) identify style and form of writing in order to reveal and express these elements within a performance
Probably seldom relevant, although it might be for teacher roles from texts, such as Morgan and Saxton's example of Claudius above.

r) use textual analysis, research and observation in the development of a role

Similar to point p.

s) study text, in both prose and verse, and make full use of the structures and phrasing in order to reveal character, intention and the development of a story

In role of King Lear the text was studied to enable the speech to draw upon the Shakespearean language for an early years drama (Ackroyd, (1998, pp35-36). Skills to study text are relevant when approaching story books for dramas.

t) create and sustain an improvised rehearsal or performance if required with discipline and spontaneity

Skills for creating and sustaining are crucial for the teacher-in-role.

u) show evidence of ability to devise and where appropriate, to direct, performance material from research and observation

We have seen above that writers identify the skills of devising and directing in teacher-in-role.

While it is clear that there are parallels, a list for training actors in noh theatre or kathakali would look very different. This list is a product of its own culture. It is born of the dominant tradition that, as I suggest, is the view of theatre held in drama in education. Broadening a view of theatre and acting will identify closer relationships with teacher-in-role. However, even in the list above, there are some points that have been identified in the literature of drama in education as important skills for teacher-in-role. Indeed, even Morgan and Saxton, who explicitly reject the notion that teacher-in-role is engaged in acting, provide a range of 'skill building exercises for teachers' which include the development of skills in role perception, signalling skills and flexibility in the use of role (1987, pp63-66).

6

APPROACHES, STYLES AND
TYPES OF ROLE

This chapter considers the ways in which acting has been distinguished from teaching in role through arguments concerning character and representation. It challenges the view that representation is the domain of teacher-in-role while becoming characters is the domain of acting. Different approaches to understanding the relationships between the actor, the role and the audience are investigated, which destabalise the seeming certainties of exponents in the field of drama in education.

Internal and external considerations

Morgan and Saxton advise that in approaching role a teacher is 'simply required to represent an attitude or point of view' (Morgan and Saxton, 1989, p49). This is clearly distinguishable from their approach to student acting, which involves 'communicating the inner life of the character' (1987, p34). This supposes that a teacher's role should not communicate an inner life. Acting is distinguished from teacher-in-role by what we might call *internal* considerations. Bolton bases much of his work on acting behaviour on Kempe's definition that 'real acting' is 'to do with developing a character' (Bolton, 1998, p195). Kempe defines acting as '... not only adopting someone else's attitudes and beliefs as in role play, but developing a sense of their character by altering the way you speak and move' (1990, p178). Here the implicit distinction be-tween role and acting focuses upon what I call *external* considera-tions. So character is identified with acting, and we see acting asso-ciated with both internal (Morgan and Saxton) and external (Kempe) features. Teacher role play appears to require neither inner life nor altered gestures.

There seem to be problems with both these views of acting. Firstly, acting is not always concerned with the inner life of the character. The Agitators in Brecht's *The Measures Taken* (1992) do not require an inner life to be communicated, nor do many commedia charac-ters. Secondly, the notion that all actors alter the way they speak and move when they act is perhaps a rather simplistic notion. Sharon Stone and Nicholas Cage play different characters but we do not see the sort of *external* changes that Kempe describes. Actors may change their voices sometimes for obvious reasons, as did the American actress playing the English character Bridget Jones. But often it is the way expression, pitch, tone and speed of language operate in particular contexts that contributes to our im-pression of the character being depicted. Voices and walks do not have to change. I have not seen Judi Dench or John Thaw 'walk' differently in different parts but when Kathryn Hunter played Lear she had a very distinctive walk as did Maggie Smith when she played the lady in Bennett's *The Lady in the Van*. Different walks and voices are not defining features of acting. Kirby would see walks or voices as 'one element or dimension of acting' (1987, p10).

Are the inner life and external changes relevant to the drama teacher-in-role? Although not experiencing the inner life, a teacher may indicate it. As the mother of an American soldier in the civil war in a drama I taught with Jonothan Neelands in Toronto (1994), I left gaps between words, fixed gazes in response to questions the children put to me, and sighs and gestures, to convey the inner life of the role. The inner life has significance in some of my teacher-in-role experiences. When I played the frightened Suzie (Ackroyd and Boulton, 2001), I moved differently because I wanted to signal my shyness. So I moved with a sideways step, with hunched shoulders and quickly moving eyes. My voice was quieter than usual and also lighter, to portray someone very young. I have seen

Jonothan Neelands teach in role in high and low status roles and have heard his voice change. A strong, flat voice as the Recruiting Sergeant (Mobbs' Boys, 1985) creates a distance between the children's roles and the high status character. As one of the troops, he dropped some consonants and softened his pitch to identify his role as one alongside the students' roles. Bolton explains how Heathcote altered her voice, '[she] often resorted to thickening her accent, using slang, even swearing (mildly!). In America her voice would often become Americanised' (Bolton 2001, letter). I must conclude that voice and movement changes are not essential for the actor, but nor are they irrelevant to the teacher-in-role.

Representation and presentation

The use of these terms is often confusing. There seems to be some difference in the ways they are used. Sometimes representation seeks to imply *indicating* as opposed to *becoming*. Representation suggests not needing to transform into what is being represented, but signifying something. However, representation is also associated with representational theatre, which implies something quite different. Here we assume the theatre represents a copy of life. Consequently, we would expect to see actors becoming rather than indicating. We associate representational theatre with naturalism and realism. Presentational theatre acknowledges the presence of an audience, so actors can address the audience. This contrasts with the second notion of representational theatre in which life is replicated with the pretence that no one is watching. I wish to consider how the concept of representation is applied in drama in education and then examine three theatrical models which might enhance our understanding of what is taking place with teacher roles.

Morgan and Saxton have constructed a list of instructions for teaching in role, under the heading 'Representing'. Here representation seems to mean indicating rather than becoming. Their example of Lister is from a drama described in *Dorothy Heathcote: Collected Writings on Education and Drama* (O'Neill (ed) 1984, pp 126-137).

Select those signals you will use to **represent** the role to your students:

Consider language: heightened and formalised for Lister

Consider costume: sleeves rolled up

Consider props: drying your hands on a towel...

Consider space: a formal set-up with a table

Consider light: the table will be placed by the window

As you and your students become more confident in working imaginatively, physical **representation** may become less necessary as they (and you) grow more capable of working symbolically.'

(My emphasis, Morgan and Saxton, 1987, p62)

Given that these writers stipulate that teacher-in-role and acting are not the same, this list should be very different from the approach taken by an actor. I asked actor Simon Callow to have a look at it. I edited it slightly to avoid the use of the words student and teacher. My question was: 'Do you think there is anything missing in this list of notes for an actor?' He read the list and explained that costume and space are not always relevant and confirmed that language is crucial (remember that in the literature highlighted in chapter 5 on skills, exactly the same is said for teachers-in-role). Callow thought that the list described what an actor does appropriately and couldn't think of anything that should be added to the list. So if we understand that the list does indeed describe what teachers do in role, then we must conclude that teachers in role do the same as Callow thinks he does as an actor. Callow's final comment on the list was that it is useful because 'it doesn't pretend that acting is just a representation of reality' (2000). I took this to mean that it doesn't simply imply realistic acting. Here we have Morgan and Saxton using 'representation' to mean not realistic, and Callow using 'a representation of reality' to mean realistic.

So Morgan and Saxton's list is titled 'Representing'. They say this is not acting, it is teacher-in-role. I have suggested that, rather than not acting, it is a different kind of acting. Callow sees the list as describing acting and that it could include non-realistic acting. What constitutes non-realistic acting might well be described by some writers as presentational acting i.e. acknowledging an audience.

However, given that teacher-in-role inevitably presupposes an acknowledgement of an audience, albeit participants, such 'representing' could be seen as 'presentational'.

Perhaps it is reductive to maintain that we will be able to identify all teacher-in-role as one of two positions, representation or presentation. This seeming opposition between representational and presentational theatre modes is not the only way to consider approaches to acting. I wish to cite three examples of other approaches which may help us here and again when understanding the practice of the case studies. We turn first to Beckerman.

Beckerman's model: direct and indirect presentation

This distinction suggests that one form of theatre involves direct communication with the audience while the other does not. It is here, in discussing representational style, that critics tend to isolate drama from the performing process, denying the fact that in a true sense, all drama is presentational. Even the most introverted, self-contained scene is intended for performance, and to the degree that it is prepared and an audience brought to witness it, it is a work of presentation (1990, pp110-111).

Beckerman proposes an alternative model for looking at the relationship between actor, role and audience. He suggests we consider direct and indirect forms of presentation. In direct presentation,

The performer acknowledges the presence of the audience and presents the show making that acknowledgement explicit. This type of playing differs from the *indirect* form of presentation where the performer supposedly does not 'admit' the presence of an audience and acts as though the activity performed has an autonomous existence. *(1990, p111)*

In contrast,

Direct presentation ... is an open exchange between performer and spectator. But drama, by its very definition, has a double nature. In performing drama, the actor assumes an identity, plays a fictional role, or does both. There is thus the actor and the act, which are fundamentally at odds with each other. The result, for direct presentation, is that openness of a dramatic actor is a sham. It is another illusion, but an illusion that proclaims it is what it appears to be. (*ibid*)

Beckerman argues that there 'is no razor sharp separation between direct and indirect presentation. All sorts of modifications of both types appear' (1990, p111). He talks of prologues and monologues which are direct addresses to the audience that have been used as conventions or as frames for a production throughout theatre history. He cites Tom Wingwood's narration in *The Glass Menagerie* as an example of the latter. Interesting because the plays of Williams are often categorised as realist. Williams' initial plan included special effects to create 'non-realistic projections' (1977, Synopsis of scenes), and the play is framed by Tom Wingwood's narration to the audience. He sets scenes for us and therefore focuses the way we, the audience, will experience them. 'In a sense he is a ringmaster or master of ceremonies' (Beckerman, 1990, p123). The example serves to illustrate the complexities of classification.

So from Beckerman we find a sense in which all theatre is presentational, and we can identify *direct* and *indirect* performances, but we can also find many performances which mix both forms of presentation. I am using Beckerman as an alternative theoretical lens to by-pass the oppositional vocabulary that distinguishes role from acting. In teacher-in-role we may well find a mix of direct and indirect presentation. If we conceptualise the children as audience rather than other actors, we can see that as soon as a teacher-in-role speaks directly to the class, she is acknowledging the audience and therefore creating a direct presentational approach.

Aston and Savona's model: three modes of representation

We turn now to a model set out in Aston and Savona's *Theatre as a Sign System*. They propose three different performance modes related to ideological positions. The first is *Conventionalised representation*, which they associate with the *classic text*. They suggest that in open air theatre 'the actor-in-role functioned as a sign of the personated character' (p46). The character is 'a function of action and of the thematic and ideological underpinnings of action' (p34). Thus the character traits are connected with the action. The second mode is *Analogical representation*, associated with *bourgeois text* in which the actor worked to identify herself with the character. The audience is thus positioned to identify the actor with the character, too. This corresponds with the development of interest in psychology and a greater interest in characters for themselves, and is therefore prevalent in nineteenth century theatrical developments and informs Stanislavski's system. The third mode, related to the *radical text*, is *Deconstructive representation*. Here characters are 're/presented as character, i.e. as construct' (p35). The characters appear to know that they are part of a performance; they often break the audience/performance space conventions. Aston and Savona argue the familiar point that in this mode the audience 'is placed at a critical remove from the action and, in consequence, from the likelihood of reflexive acts of emotional identification with the characters. Hence, a more active mode of spectatorship is placed on offer' (p36).

This model provides another useful lens for looking at teacher-in-role as it offers a distinction between types of distanced role. Firstly, there is the distance that is the *conventionalised representation*. There is some degree of identification with the role and yet this is conventionalised. There are conventions within which children interpret the signs of their teacher-in-role. They know not to expect costumes and make-up. There is no visual realism; the teacher looks like who she was at register, yet she appears to believe in her role. Aston and Savona provide a model enabling us to examine another mode of distanced performance which could be applicable to classroom drama. If the teacher role player is distinct from the role, she may be at a 'critical remove' from it as defined by *deconstructive representation*. This is where the distance between actor and role is deliberate and made explicit. The duality is part of the performance encounter. In role I have operated in this mode. I have made a statement that I know has relevance to our shared 'real lives' as well as in the fiction. Often it is a little joke for us as players. Occasionally children do the same thing so that a reference has dual relevance. It serves to remind us all of the duality and therefore clearly deconstructs the pretend.

These three modes make clear distinctions between two types of 'distanced' role and thus enable us to identify those moments of playfulness in our practice. In role a teacher may also make an aside which is deconstructing the pretend by making a comment which has a serious intention regarding the shared 'real life'.

States' model: expressive, collaborative and representational modes

Let us now turn to Bert O. States' chapter, *The Actor's Presence: Three phenomenal modes*, which proposes a view of the actor as a story teller 'whose speciality is that he is the story he is telling' (1996, p22). States proposes three modes in which the actor can speak to the audience. The first is the self-expressive mode, the second the collaborative mode and the third the representational mode. 'In the self expressive mode the actor *seems* to be performing on his own behalf. He says in effect, '*See what I can do.*' ...the moment when artistry becomes the object of our attention' (p26). He does not simply mean that we, the audience, recognise the actor, but that we recognise the artistry: 'we react to the actor's particular way of doing his role' (p26). States suggests that there are certain parts which were written to display the prowess of particular actors and therefore are almost inevitably operating in this mode. He argues that some roles 'encourage the self-expressive tendency (Cyrano, Faust, Falstaff, Hamlet, Lear, Medea)' (p24). It is clear that Morgan and Saxton do not intend their teachers to take this approach to role. When they require teachers 'not' to act and 'not' to be a performer, it is probably because they do not believe that a teacher role should be carried out in what States calls a 'self-expressive mode'. Throughout the literature of drama in education we have seen the articulated aim as being something other than drawing attention to the self or the teacher's performance skills. There may have been a sense that this would avoid 'acting', but States' distinctions of the actor's mode may be helpful in clarifying this as just one type of approach to acting.

The collaborative mode aims to 'break down the distance between actor and audience and to give the spectator something more than a passive role in the theatre exchange. The invitation to collaborate varies from the 'implicit to explicit, and from the token to the literal' (p29). Such collaborative moments will include examples cited in the discussion of presentational theatre. There is often a sense that the actor plays a character who lives in a world that includes the audience. It can be a play including just one character who does this, such as Tom Wingfield – to keep to our example of *The Glass Menagerie* – or the few characters in Shakespeare who soliloquise whereas the others do not. Equally, in pantomime characters acknowledge the audience. States articulates the difference between the audience in neo classical tragedy that has the status 'of a sort of *confidant* character ...unlike the ''real' audience that modern participation theatre tries to involve quite literally in the play' (p29). A Peepolikus production entitled *Goosebumps* (1999) required members of the audience to vote on a decision and some were drawn into the performance space to create one of the scenes. States explains that he

> originally thought of the Brechtian actor as performing primarily in the self-expressive mode because he was, to a noticeable degree, still a performer standing just outside of his role. But this is not really self-expressiveness...this detachment, or coming forth, of the Brechtian actor is a strategy for keeping the spectator on the objective wave-length in his 'hearing' of the play. (p31)

The distinguishing characteristic States employs to identify the collaborative mode is the form of the 'you' address in relation to the audience. 'One could think of this as a 'we' voice in the sense that the audience joins the actors in the stage enterprise' (*ibid*), but States prefers to remain with the 'you' voice. Both comply with what would take place in Morgan and Saxton's teacher role-play. The participant audience will be addressed as 'you' and there may also be uses of 'we'. What is required of the teacher-in-role could be seen as a collaborative mode of speaking to the audience/ participants.

Behind the third mode, the 'representational mode of performance, and our perception of it, is the shared sense that we come to the theatre primarily to see a play, not a performance'. Here we

> look in objectively on a 'drama' with a beginning, middle and end that is 'occurring' before our eyes. All of the actor's artistic energies now seem to be bent toward 'becoming' his character ... the audience simply sees through the 'sign language' of the art to the signified' beyond. So the virtuosity now lies in the power of the subject, the collaboration in the mutual agreement by actor and audience on the value and appropriateness of the subject to the community of men. (p35)

States goes to great length to explain that his representational mode of performance does not imply a 'realistic' style of production. 'What we call realism is no closer to reality than many forms of representation we would call stylised' (p36). He is also at pains to emphasise that although he uses the three modes distinctly as a convenience, he is not saying that in theatre they are not frequently cohabiting. 'There is no incompatibility among the modes: they co-exist continuously' (p35).

Different approaches and different roles

Strasberg maintained that 'There are two kinds of acting. One believes that the actor can actually experience on the stage. The other believes that the actor only indicates what the actor experiences, but does not himself really experience' (1991, p144-145). Vasiliev's ludo system places the actor outside the character, not in a Brechtian sense since he worked outside a socio-political context, but in contrast to what he describes as the psychological system that assumes the actor is inside the character played. However, the most frequently cited approaches to acting in the western educational contexts are those established by Stanislavski and Brecht. The system Stanislavski laid out in *An Actor Prepares* (1993) has been a consistent part of actor training in spirit, if not to the letter. The approach to role described by Brecht in 'The Street Scene' (1986, pp121-126) suggests something quite different.

There is room for actors to implement different approaches for different plays. Simon Callow is clear about the way he approached his role when performing in *Fanshen*. He contrasts it with the approach required for performing the psychologist in *Mary Barnes*, which required a more involved form of acting. Callow explains that in *Fanshen* the particular characters are not important and thus the actor should not be psychologically engaged (Callow, 1985). This is logical. The characters have been given no names but represent archtypes such as 'peasant'. Callow says of his work in *Fanshen*, 'I was just saying to the audience, 'Ladies and gentlemen, this kind of person exists.' When I spoke to him he compared this to the way he had performed Masha in *Three Sisters*. 'I tried to offer an x ray of her heart' (2000).

Perhaps similar distinctions can be made in the roles that teachers play. If the teacher role is the newspaper editor in Neelands' drama (Neelands, 1993), then the character is irrelevant. Just as in *Fanshen* the character needs no name, the editor remains 'the editor'. Perhaps then Neelands' role was played simply with an awareness of what the role represented, i.e. standards in news articles, giving no consideration to being a character, a personality. In contrast, Lamont and Readman's teacher-in-role appears as a child frightened to go to school (1994). Likewise the role I play of an anxious girl who is afraid to go out in the snow because of an accident the previous year. The children meet a character called Suzie (Ackroyd, 1994) who has a way of avoiding questions which tug at her fears, as well as being quite full of herself and a tomboy. It is through gradually understanding the strengths and weaknesses of her personality that children begin to address her problem. When I play this role, I am aware that I need to create a character. She is not just a small girl; she is Suzie, just as Masha is Masha, an individual character in a particular context. My preparation has never been a deep psychological one, and I have never considered fears in my own experience. My Suzie might be described as *direct representation,* as it involved a direct approach to the audience/children. It was operating in the *collective* mode since an active part was expected and, indeed, demanded of that audience/children. Was I becoming the character or was I, in Mamet's terms, just 'communicating the play'?

> The actor does not need to 'become' the character. The phrase, in fact, has no meaning. There *is* no character. There are only lines upon a page. They are lines of dialogue meant to be said by an actor. And the actor is onstage to communicate the play to the audience. That is the beginning and the end of his and her job. (Mamet, 1997, p9 original emphasis)

This view of a delivery role for the actors is considered dated by many who see 'actors as artists in their own right rather than 'mouthpieces' for the playwright's words' (Neelands and Dobson, 2000b, p211). However, with the influence of post-structuralism there is a view that character does not 'exist' in real life, the actor therefore cannot 'become' that character on stage. For semioticians, the character is no more or less than a set of signs. These signs are variable, since they are determined by the actor in the context of the production. Ian Holme's King Lear was thus very different from Nigel Hawthorne's – as were both from Katherine Hunter's.

It is clear then that actors are not always expected to 'become' the characters they are playing and, indeed, not all roles presented are full-blooded characters. Many are roles in the sense that they perform as a social function, such as a worker, rich man, mother, politician. Often with no names beyond the label that determines that social function, the role is defined more quickly than a named character that we gradually get to know and understand. Such theatre is associated with expressionistic and Brechtian conventions and has an explicit socio-political agenda. I can recognise similar distinctions of role type in my own teacher roles. I have played the factory owner's spokesperson who is signified and relevant only in terms of her role as spokesperson for the factory owner. In contrast, Suzie is met by the children as just a young girl who is sad. The discovery of her accident in the snow the previous year is significant as the character and context of Suzie is gradually revealed. She has no particular social role that makes sense of the dramatic fiction. The social learning about resolving problems and supporting peers comes after the discovery of who Suzie is and what has befallen her.

I began this chapter by asking what kinds of approaches are required of teachers and actors. I suggested that the Morgan and Saxton description defines what teacher-in-role should do by describing what an actor should do, according to actor and writer Simon Callow. I have looked at views of representation as located in opposition to presentation. In seeking alternatives to seeing representational and presentational performance as polarised, three different models for approaching role have been provided and consideration given to how they elucidate the theory and practice of teaching in role. Also discussed were the different approaches that might be made with different roles both on stage and in the classroom, and the way that the portrayal of the same roles varies with the individuality of the role taker. It is already clear that the same critical models can be applied to both teacher-in-role and acting, and these will aid analysis in the case studies that follow.

7

TOWARDS A REVISED MODEL OF
TEACHER-IN-ROLE

This chapter explores two areas. Firstly: the assumptions about
theatre and acting revealed through the review of literature on
drama in education. This points to the need for a broader view of
both theatre and acting, which in turn demands a redraft of the
Categorising Teacher-in-role and Actor: The First Model (Table 1)
in chapter 1. Secondly: the possible reasons for the assumptions
outlined. I draw support from historical evidence about public perceptions of actors and upon documented evidence concerning a
theatre-drama rift in the 1940s, and I consider why the assumptions of the past may have continued.

What assumptions have been held?

In the Preface of *Beginning Drama: 11-14* (1998) Jonothan Neelands describes the type of theatre that he believes exists in the
popular imagination.

> It is a picture of theatre that is based on an economic agreement
> between the producers of theatre and the audience. The pro-
> ducers rehearse and develop a theatre product to the best of
> their abilities and, when the time comes, they perform their
> work in exchange for the price of a ticket. (viii)

More often than not the product that is exchanged is based on the
work of a playwright. The assumption in this model of theatre is

that the majority of us will see, rather than be in, such plays. Acting, producing theatre, is seen as something only a few can achieve. There is also the assumption that the audience in this literary theatre will be silent and attentive to the work of the actors – audience responses are private rather than publicly shared as in more popular forms of entertainment. I describe theatre that corresponds to this image as belonging to the 'literary and private aesthetic tradition' (Neelands, 1998). But there are alternative models of community theatre and performance which may bring us closer to seeing teacher-in-role as acting.

This crystallises much of what I have been arguing in this section. The 'common sense' view which has led to specific assumptions about acting is a dominant view of theatre. We can identify the assumptions within the field of drama in education (see box opposite).

Many of these assumptions are used to distance teacher-in-role from acting. However, with a broader view of theatre and acting, a distinction between teacher-in-role and acting becomes more difficult to sustain. I have discussed alternative models of theatre and acting to those implied in the literature of drama in education. Boal's actors challenge these assumptions, as do actors in street theatre, commedia and pantomime.

So a list of commonalities which may have read as:

Teachers-in-role and actors both
> communicate through sign
> operate in fictional time
> operate in imagined space
> speak in the 'here and now'
> have a captive audience
> structure rhythm and pace to keep others' attention
> carry out planned work
> speak as someone other than themselves

might now be extended to include

> deal with intervention
> adapt to the responses to their work
> may adopt different language registers

ACTING INVOLVES

An awareness of audience	Being able to 'read us and work with the energy of the audience' (Morgan and Saxton, 1989, p34)
Inner life of characters	'communicating the inner life of the character' (*ibid*)
	'representing the character to the audience' (*ibid*)
Developing a character	'real acting...is to do with developing a character' (Bolton, 1998, p195)
Changing voice and movement	'not only adopting someone's beliefs as in role play, but developing a sense of their character by altering the way you speak and move' (Kempe, 1990, p178)
Costumes	'teacher-in-role is not about acting in the external sense of putting on a costume and finding a voice and set of mannerisms for a character' (Bowell and Heap, 2001, p47)
Gestures	Being able to 'convey subtleties of nuance and gesture' (Morgan and Saxton, 1989, p34)
No spontaneity	Being 'no longer free to shift around spontaneously' (*ibid* p35)
Script	'Those involved...were caught up in a dramatic experience that they created and maintained yet which possessed no prior script, fixed scenario, or separate audience' (O'Neill, conversation 2000)
Expectation of applause	'This tacit invitation from the actor for approval from an audience' (Bolton, conversation 2001)

may adopt particular gestures

have particular intentions

Let us revisit the Categorising TIR and Actor Grid: The First Model (Table 1) in chapter 1 (p5). In the original list the descriptors are different for the teacher-in-role and the actor, but in this revised grid alternative forms of theatre are identified which move the actor's situation closer to that of the teacher-in-role. My alterations in the light of this section are in bold (see table 2, p73-74).

In every case there is an example of some theatre form that blurs the boundaries between the experience of teacher-in-role and actor.

Why these assumptions?

Several possible reasons have led to the assumption that teacher-in-role is not acting. Because of the somewhat restricted view of theatre, a similarly restricted view of the actor inevitably followed. I can suggest four further reasons why these assumptions may have been held.

Actors are undesirable – there are many sources where the historically low status of the actor has been recorded.

> Remember that acting was once considered to be a very lowly and dubious occupation. The first actors in fifth-century Athens were called hypocrites, meaning 'answerer' or 'interpreter', from which we get the word 'hypocrite', meaning someone false or duplicitous. In the early days of the travelling theatre companies in America, actors were buried at the crossroads with a stake in their hearts. (Neelands and Dobson, 2000b, p9)

Not only in the west has suspicion of actors prevailed. Throughout history and across cultures there has been discomfort with the ambiguity between what is real and what is fictional. So while we know that 'in Rome acting was felt to be the work of slaves and aliens ... in modern Europe players long existed on the margins of law and religion' (*The Cambridge Guide to Theatre*, 1995, p4), similar dubious status was awarded actors in the East. In Asia performers 'were and often still are, equated with wanderers and beggars ... In China, decrees dating from as early as 1369 banned actors from entering for state examinations' (*ibid*).

Table 2: REVISED CATEGORISING TIR/ACTOR GRID: THE SECOND MODEL

	TEACHER-IN-ROLE	ACTOR
Overall power in the in the experience	the teacher is privileged	the audience is privileged

In forum theatre it is the actor

	TEACHER-IN-ROLE	ACTOR
Content	chosen by teacher	given to the actor

In devised theatre it is often chosen by the actor(s)

	TEACHER-IN-ROLE	ACTOR
Intention	to fulfil learning objectives	to entertain

Theatre for health education, TIE and Brecht's lehrstucke *have the intention to teach*

	TEACHER-IN-ROLE	ACTOR
Responsibility for audience welfare and behaviour	fully and legally responsible	no responsibility

In community theatre, the actor might take responsibility and in murder mystery theatre, the 'audience' are customers and must be 'looked after' by the company

	TEACHER-IN-ROLE	ACTOR
Audience attendance	compulsory	voluntary

Theatre in Education is usually compulsory for the children who attend

	TEACHER-IN-ROLE	ACTOR
Audience expectation	to learn (to be bored/ interested?)	to be entertained (to be challenged /amused?)

Theatres for development and health perform to audiences who expect to be taught something useful as well as be entertained

	TEACHER-IN-ROLE	ACTOR
Audience role	active participation	inactive participation

Active in Boal's forum theatre and commercial forms of interactive theatre/entertainment such as murder mystery theatre and pantomime

continued...

	TEACHER-IN-ROLE	ACTOR
Audience relationships	familiar	unfamiliar

Familiar in community theatre and often in Theatre in Education

	TEACHER-IN-ROLE	ACTOR
Audience size	small group	large group

Small in many applied theatre contexts, in prisons and theatre for very young children

	TEACHER-IN-ROLE	ACTOR
Audience age	school age	mixed, usually a minority under 25 years

More under 25 in children's theatre, youth theatre and pantomime

	TEACHER-IN-ROLE	ACTOR
Social class of audience	in state system – mixed, often without upper middle and usually without upper class	predominantly middle class

Mixed in street theatre, educational theatre, theatre for prisons and theatre for development

	TEACHER-IN-ROLE	ACTOR
Selection of role	can be chosen and can change at any time	given before event and cannot be changed

Not always given in improvisation and theatre sports and requires constant change of role on the part of the actor

	TEACHER-IN-ROLE	ACTOR
Response to audience reaction	flexibility to adapt and challenge audience assumptions	no verbal flexibility, no possibility to respond

In improvised theatre – Johnstone's, commedia, pantomime

	TEACHER-IN-ROLE	ACTOR
Environment	school hall/classroom	theatre space

Not always in a theatre – prisons, streets, village halls, school halls

If actors had low status, women actors have been the lowest of the low. Women did not act in England until after the Restoration and even then 'no woman with serious pretensions to respectability would countenance a stage career' (Howe, 1992, p32).

Alison Oddey's playful choice of book title suggests that a dubious view of women actors remains: *Performing Women: Stand-Ups, Strumpets and Itinerants* (1999).

Wariness of actors and an assumption that their moral codes are loose lingers in the UK. There are many personal testaments to evidence the negative view of actors, such as June Whitfield's anecdote: 'The funny thing is that my grandfather would not allow my mother to go on the stage. He thought actors were all rogues and mountebanks' (1999, p215). Actors are not seen to be like others and are simply not deemed trustworthy (Harrop,1992 and Neelands, 1998b). Teachers, on the other hand, must be deemed trustworthy and responsible. They have always been required to at least appear to be above immorality, scandal and even bad manners. The role of educating children, it seems, requires a particular demeanour. Heathcote hints at a view of actor mannerisms as almost uncouth in an educational context: 'Coming from the theatre also, you don't consider sign to be bad manners. I still meet colleagues who somehow manage by their signing, to indicate to me that there is something rather ungenteel about behaving like that in classrooms' (1980). It is no wonder that there has been a desire to distance the work of teachers from that of actors.

The drama and theatre rift – the distinction between acting and teacher-in-role may be associated with the development of drama in education. When the drama in education movement began to develop there was a need to map itself a distinct identity. Of the famous conference at the Bonnington Hotel, John Allen wrote, 'Here, for the first time, I realised, with an alarm I can recall to this day, the depth of the split that was developing between concepts of drama in schools and theatre arts' (1979, p12). And of the First Conference on Youth and Theatre a year later, Redington recalled that 'the distinction between techniques of creative dramatics and formal dramatics, or the production and performance of plays before an audience' was foregrounded (Redington, cited in Lewick,

1996). This distinction was crucial for drama in education to develop. Peter Slade's vision for children's theatre meant that changes were made. The terminology changed, too. Slade introduced the term 'child drama' (1958) and the now familiar term, drama in education was coined. These alternative labels reasserted a distinction from theatre. When the term theatre was not applied to class drama, the word acting would not be heard in relation to the children or the teacher. If the children and their teachers were acting, the approach would be equated with what people do on the stage and not as the fresh innovative practice it was.

The search for universal truths and authenticity – the major practitioners of drama in education see themselves as 'deepening understanding' (Bolton, 1979, p105) and enabling children to 'finish up thinking more deeply or rationally or intelligently about the subject' (*ibid* p92). Given this concern to justify drama in education in terms of its unique contribution to cognitive development, there has been a reluctance to see drama as in some way dealing with the fictional. Best writes

> The notion of 'fiction' is also problematic. In a very common sense, to say that something is a fiction is to say that it is false, even a lie, whereas Gavin [Bolton] and I want to emphasise the vital potential of drama/theatre to reveal truths. To say that drama deals with the fictional may well contribute to the depressingly prevalent assumption that it is concerned with fantasy, escapism, what is not true. (2001, p11)

As fiction and truth may be seen as problematic partners, so, too, are acting and truth. Drama teachers see themselves exploring issues that are *real* and have *real* significance. An ironic paradox emerges. Since acting is associated with falsehood, it could not be deemed appropriate for the worthy and serious endeavours of classroom drama. It could be argued that there has been a residual Puritanism about the attitude towards actors and that this has seeped into the mindset of drama in education practitioners. With the elevation of sincerity as a principle public virtue (Sennett, 1977) acting, being by nature deceitful, presents a problem. Acting in common sense terms could not be expected to provide a way to truth and sincerity.

Simplifying the practice. When encouraging teachers or students to use it, it has been perceived as a definite advantage to see teacher-in-role as not acting. In an attempt to make the task sound less daunting, when training teachers, I have asserted that you don't have to act to work in role. For many teachers, the idea of acting is off-putting, if not for the reasons discussed, then simply because they assume they cannot act and feel that trying to do so will be embarrassing. John O'Toole writes in an email about his early work in Australia with student teachers: 'I was careful to stress that teacher-in-role did not have to be showy, nor did you have to be an actor. Horses for courses, of course, but looking back, and reading my notes of the time, I think I undersold the theatre and acting implicit in the mode' (2002). We are all keen to encourage more teachers to use teacher-in-role and yet the very idea of it often scares even the toughest of teachers. So our reassurance that it is not acting became a mantra.

SECTION TWO
CASE STUDIES

8
INTRODUCING THE CASE STUDIES

The case study drama education practitioners were selected on grounds of their contributions to the field of drama in education and their significance in terms of international influence through both theoretical and practical work. Actor Fiona Shaw's published interviews interested me and I have long admired her work.

There were obviously differences between the teacher and actor encounters. Drama teachers assume some degree of understanding of what actors do and are therefore able to discuss their ideas for comparison, but Shaw could not be expected to know what I meant by teacher-in-role. Similarly, I was much more familiar with the teachers and their work than with the actor and hers.

The following three chapters relate the three case studies. Each chapter is organised in the same way, in eight stages:

• introduction to case study subject

• narrative account of the session observed

• semiotic analysis of the session

• an over view of the interview

• analysis of the interview

• a contextualisation of the case study in the light of Section One

• comment.

The introductions to Cecily O'Neill and John O'Toole are based on emailed responses to three questions: How did you discover teacher-in-role? What or who has most influenced your work? What would you say has been your main contribution to the field of drama education? Since readers may be less familiar with the work of Fiona Shaw there is a longer introduction to it, based on articles and interviews. The narrative account explains what took place in the drama. This enables readers to use the dramas themselves if they choose. The semiotic system for analysing each of the case study observations is described below. In unstructured interviews after the observed sessions, I tried to glean a sense of the views of each of the practitioners about what they are doing. The most relevant extracts of the interview are quoted, but not necessarily in the order in which they were said, as I have edited their comments to draw particular points together. The interview analysis explores the assumptions that seem to lie behind each practitioner's thinking. Here, informed by the research into assumptions discussed in Section One, I am concerned with the values that shape views that often appear to be unquestioned. Next I consider the practice in the light of the theoretical examinations of Section One. Finally, the findings of the case study are brought together and a range of questions posed.

Semiotic analysis

In order to analyse the practice I observed, I decided on a semiotic approach. Semiotics or semiology 'is concerned primarily, with how meaning is generated in 'texts'. It deals with signs and how they function' (Berger, 1991, [1933], p14). The term 'semiology' was introduced by Saussure in 1915 (1966, p16). Aston and Savona argue the case for viewing theatre semiotics 'not as a theoretical position but as a *methodology*: as a way of working, of approaching theatre in order to open up new practices and possibilities of 'seeing'' (1991, p1). I wanted to use semiotics as a way of seeing, of sensitising my observation to what I may otherwise have missed. It also provided me with a systematic language which would provide 'a base from which to assess what we have seen' (*ibid* p5).

I approached the preparation of a semiotic framework aware that a semiotic approach has many concerns and limitations. Firstly, as Esslin notes, 'the obscure language and excessively abstract way in which the, in many cases, outstandingly brilliant exponents of semiotics [present] their findings' (1987, p11). Secondly, there is the fact that theatre does not stand still while an observer takes in every sign that exists at any one moment in time. Inevitably, some members of an audience will catch different signs from others (Harrop, 1992). Thirdly, there is the problem, identified somewhat brutally by Jonathan Miller, that 'both critics and audience are led to over-interpret gestures and expressions and read meanings into movements that had no significance whatever' (1972, p365). This is certainly the case. Kier Elam explains that

> The audience starts with the assumptions that every detail is an intentional sign and whatever cannot be related to the representation as such is converted into a sign of the actor's very reality – it is not, in any case, excluded from semiosis. (1991, p9)

But what attracted me was the specific insights semiotics could offer an understanding of the actor, and in my project, the teacher-in-role. The actor herself is 'the dynamic unity of an entire set of signs' (Veltrusky, 1940, p84). '...the actor's body acquires its mimetic and representational powers by becoming something other than itself, more and less than individual. This applies equally to his speech (which assumes the general signified 'discourse') and to every aspect of his performance' (Elam, 1991, p9). In the case studies, taking note of the oral text of the teacher-in-role and actor would be inadequate.

> A linguistic utterance is not simply a product of the phonological, syntactic and semantic rules of the language. As we have seen, contextual constraints and the kinds of language-related behaviour accompanying the utterance are essential to its correct interpretation by the addressee. Intimately related to the speaker's parakinesic 'orchestrating' of the discourse are vocal characteristics with which he endows it over and above its phonemic and syntactic structure...Such features supply essential information regarding the speaker's state, intentions and attitudes, serving further (in conjunction with kinesic factors) to disambiguate the speech act. (Elam, 1991, p79)

I have been influenced by Elam's approach to breaking down the actor's ways of producing signs, such as body and voice and the paralinguistic repertory (*ibid* p32-97). I drew on his work to construct the semiotic system of analysis used in the three case studies. If semiotics can illuminate 'how meaning is created and communicated through systems of encodable and decodable signs' (Aston and Savona, 1991, p3) in the theatre, it might be able to do the same for teacher-in-role.

I apply two semiotic models to deconstruct the action in the case studies. The first provides a detailed semiotic analysis of the session as a whole, taking generalisations at each stage to see if any patterns can be identified. It highlights the various ways in which meaning is transmitted. These range from the words spoken, to the costume and properties, as indicated below. It is thus possible to note differences between the teacher herself and the roles she takes.

Transmitters	Teacher	Role A	Role B
Oral text			
Paralinguistic features			
Kinesic factors			
Proxemic relations			
Vestimentary codes			
Properties			

The second focuses on a particular moment in the drama and enables a thorough semiotic inspection of that moment. The table provides an interpretation of both the encoding and decoding taking place in the selected moment of drama.

Encoding of meaning				Decoding of meaning		
Source of information	Oral text	Paralinguistic register	Kinesic factors	Meaning	Intention	Desired audience reaction

Both semiotic enquiries bring to light different understandings and these are explained in the context of each case study.

9

Case study – CECILY O'NEILL

Cecily O'Neill began working in schools in London, initially teaching English and then drama. She was Warden of the Inner London Education Authority's Drama and Tape Centre, where she ran in-service courses for teachers between 1974 and 1986. The co-authored *Drama Guidelines and Drama Structures* (1976 and 1982) are products of this era. O'Neill later co-edited *Dorothy Heathcote: Collected Writings on Education and Drama* (1984). From London she moved to the Ohio State University in 1987 where she stayed until 2000. As Associate Professor of Drama Education she taught post-graduate courses and supervised students taking MA and PhD courses. *Drama Worlds: A Framework for Process Drama* (1995) was published during her time in the United States.

O'Neill began to use teacher-in-role having seen Heathcote and Bolton demonstrate the approach in the seventies. She says that she 'tried to emulate Dorothy, but became too controlling, and the kids often got rid of [her]' (interview, 2000). When she saw Bolton work, she thought that a lower-key role would suit her teaching style and capabilities better, so she began to use a 'kind of 'bureaucratic' style' (email, 2001). She used the status of the second in command because she saw that such a person is not worth opposing.

Although she was 'inspired by the work of Heathcote' and 'thrilled to work with Keith Johnstone and Veronica Sherbourne' (*ibid*),

O'Neill sees her greatest influence as Gavin Bolton. 'I did my MA
with him, but his grasp of form within process and his use of significant content produced many 'AHA!' moments, as I realised what
drama could be'(*ibid*).

O'Neill acknowledges that Drama Structures, co-authored with
Alan Lambert, has...

> been very influential and spawned many imitators. [Their] pur-
> pose in writing it was to make the kind of drama that Gavin
> and Dorothy espoused actually accessible to teachers. We felt
> we were interpreters of their approach. I feel I may have contri-
> buted to an understanding of the structure of Process Drama,
> as well as popularising the term. My aim was to convey how an
> open, episodic dramatic and largely improvised structure can
> generate a dramatic event where the episodes function as 'a
> series of segmentations each possessing a sufficient demon-
> strative power' as Barthes puts it.'(*ibid*)

CONTEXT OF OBSERVATION

When	18 March, 2000
With whom	Royal National Youth Theatre group
Duration	2 hours
Where	A large rehearsal room at the Royal National Theatre, London
Participants	Seventeen young people aged between 12 and 19 who were well acquainted with one another
Gender/ethnic mix	Thirteen girls and four boys
	all white
Space	Large space with high ceilings and long mirrors
Experience	Many had been part of the group for 18 months. All were experienced in drama
Knowledge of leader	Two had once worked with O'Neill before

Narrative account of session

The drama seemed planned to consider issues surrounding genetic engineering and the associated moral and ethical questions.

A range of warm-up activities included walking in space and introduction games. I was later told that O'Neill would not usually begin a drama in this way, but she knew that this group was used to beginning with exercises.

Stage 1

The group was arranged on chairs in a circle. O'Neill explained, 'You are all outstanding in anything of your choice'. The context was explained: the participants had been invited to a conference centre where the facilities were superb. The young people were invited to contribute ideas to create a description of the lavish conference centre and its grounds.

O'Neill moved between narration, shared planning with the group, and the role of Mrs Green, the conference convenor. Each participant created their own role, deciding what they were exceptionally good at, from whom they had received their skills and how they had developed them in their lives. Each shared these details in the form of a general introductory session to the conference. Their choices ranged from Olympic athletes to actors. At this stage it was still unclear what the conference was actually about, but they knew they were there because something set them apart from others.

Stage 2

O'Neill's narration informed the group that it was now the following morning. The conference delegates were well rested etc. O'Neill then took on the role of Mrs Green again and stumblingly, hesitantly informed the group that it wasn't her fault or her responsibility, but she had been told to inform them that they were all clones. The delegates questioned and challenged Mrs Green. They found it hard to believe and seemed upset. They were unable to discover much information from Mrs Green, who was apparently not in a position to know all the details. She was after all 'just doing her job'. When they wanted to use the telephone to check the claims with their families, they were warned not to make any calls out of the conference centre – 'you know what the newspapers are like'. They were told that the work on their cloning had all happened long before Dolly the sheep was brought to public attention. At this point the participants learned that the conference centre was owned by the Institute of Human Potential Development.

Stage 3
O'Neill asked the participants what they thought about the events. Each spoke in the role of a clone. The clones were asked what they would say to their originators, given the opportunity.

Mrs Green gave out a second piece of information: the company is considering the fact that if an originator was sixty years old now, then the genetic material that had been used to create the delegates would be that age. This meant that at an age of twenty-four, the sprinter might be made up of sixty year old genetic material. The participants asked more questions, and their voices and expressions suggested that they were becoming angry and/or upset.

Stage 4
The participants changed role and were addressed as the originators, 'You agreed some while ago to donate genetic material'. They claimed no responsibility, and said that the whole affair had been mishandled. The originators were as unhappy as the clones.

Stage 5
Pair work followed, to show a clone meeting 'its' originator. O'Neill's narration, suggesting that the truth of the cloning had been leaked to the media, concluded the session.

Additional note
At the end of the session O'Neill invited me to tell the young people why I was observing and asked them if they thought she was acting. A girl replied that O'Neill was not acting at the beginning of the drama but that later on she was. This comment, and O'Neill's response to it, became a significant feature of the case study.

Semiotic analysis of the session

Two points emerge from the first semiotic experiment. Firstly, it is clear that semiotic analysis can be applied to teacher-in-role to elucidate the communication process, just as it does with actors in role. Secondly, the semiotic analysis identified significant changes in the communication through role that had been barely visible at the outset. Semiotics enabled a sharper view of what had taken place. The sources of the signs transmitted in this case study are O'Neill as firstly the narrator, and also as Mrs Green at three different stages of the drama. The way O'Neill presents herself as teacher is the benchmark from which changes in signing can be identified.

The semiotic analysis reveals that there was no significant distinction between O'Neill the teacher and O'Neill the narrator. However, it identifies the distance between O'Neill the teacher and O'Neill as Mrs Green as changing during the drama. Mrs Green became progressively less like O'Neill the teacher, showing signs of emotional discomfort in stages two and three. The table charts these changes from the teacher to the narrator and congress convenor. The description in bold type indicates significant changes from the teacher.

Semiotic analysis: personas in stages 1, 2 and 3

The box on page 92 records distinguishable changes from O'Neill the teacher to O'Neill the teacher-in-role. As the tension of the drama increased, O'Neill's body and voice changed. The plot required an altered Mrs Green from the quiet, controlled woman who introduced the congress. The further into the drama, the greater the difference between teacher and Mrs Green became. The metonymic accessories (costumes, properties, etc) did not change at any point, so the role-player remained the source of communicating signs.

I have chosen to examine a moment from the later part of the session when the student may have thought that O'Neill was acting. It comes when the differences between O'Neill as teacher and as Mrs Green are greatest.

Transmitters	Teacher	Narrator	Mrs. Green Stage 1	Mrs. Green Stage 2	Mrs. Green Stage 3
Oral text	Straightforward, clear language, semi-formal register	The same, but with more descriptive language	The same, but a more formal register	The same, but a more formal register	The same, but a more formal register
Paralinguistic features	Mid range volume, regular pace, moderate pitch	The same, with slight upward inflection	The same	**Faltering, hesitant. Communicating discomfort**	**Disjointed, staccato, increased rhythm and volume. Communicating tension, distance, and some despair**
Kinesic factors	Minimal gesture, sitting still with minimal hand movement	The same	The same	**Notable gestures: hands held up by head**	**Notable gestures: palms facing up at waist height, moving up and down heavily**
Proxemic relations	On one chair in a circle of chairs for participants in the centre of the space.	The same	The same	**Standing up**	**Standing up**
Vestimentary codes	Trousers and top	The same	The same	The same	The same
Properties	None	The same	The same	The same	The same

Semiotic analysis: a moment of drama

'Decoding' refers to my interpretation of what was communicated. It may differ from the way individual participants actually decoded. This semiotic analysis enables insight into exactly what was taking place when O'Neill worked in role, and how it was communicated. Furthermore, it provides an explanation for the student's remark that O'Neill was 'acting' at the end of the drama, but not at the beginning. The semiotic categories demonstrate that at the beginning Mrs Green was like O'Neill herself in every way, calmly introducing the athletes to the conference centre just as she had calmly introduced herself to the students at the beginning of the session, as Cecily O'Neill. This may not have looked like acting to the student, because there was no significant change. A person entering the room might not have guessed that O'Neill was speaking as someone else. However, later in the drama, the semiotic analysis identifies distinctions between O'Neill the teacher and Mrs Green. There were gestures which clearly were not those of O'Neill the teacher. When her hand was on her hip and palms were upwards while giving more distressing information, we

Encoding of meaning				Decoding of meaning		
Source of information	Oral text	Paralinguistic register	Kinesic factors	Meaning	Intention	Desired audience reaction
O'Neill	'This is very difficult. This is nothing to do with me. I must tell you, but I am not involved.'	Broken rhythm, irregular pauses, clipped enunciation: faltering, stumbling, breathy, hesitating.	Palms up and out at waist height, moving up and down heavily	I am not comfortable with what I have to say. Don't blame me.	Emphasise the injustice of what has taken place.	Look beyond Mrs Green to the implications and issues.

all knew that if O'Neill stopped at that moment and spoke as herself, her arms would drop and her palms face to her sides.

The interview

O'Neill contrasted teacher-in-role and acting as follows:

> I've always seen it as a rather functional thing where you adopt a role in drama particularly, but you present an attitude or display a point of view or a perspective... I see it as marginally different to what the actor does. The actor, I feel, inhabits a role more fully, or a character more fully, because they know in advance the full extent of their character's history. They know the character's journey'.

This implies a distinction between improvised drama and drama developed from an agreed, pre-planned text. O'Neill said that her role was different from the latter because she did not know Mrs Green's journey, just the beginning and a few points on the way...

> but I see it as being a fairly superficial kind of acting, if it is acting, because it mustn't draw attention. I have no interest in it drawing attention to any personal and internal qualities that Mrs Green might be supposed to have, so I see her as extremely functional.

When I suggested that we saw Mrs Green looking guilty about the news she had to give, and that this perhaps suggested an internal existence, she replied

> No. That's functional. That's her trying to get off the hook by saying 'I was only doing my job' ...It's functional because for the very reason that she doesn't want to be the person taking the blame... so all of those defensive tactics may look like character, but actually, they are also teacher functions or indeed playwright functions if you want to say that.

O'Neill's constant concern is that if the children become interested in the person of Mrs Green, she will have failed in the drama because 'actually, I want to distance beyond her to the scientist or whoever... If I get interested in the character I am playing, the role I'm playing, then I've sort of failed because then it's going to be about me'. She talked of the types of roles she played in the past, calling them as 'heavy' roles. They were people in control who were eventually 'got rid of ... there was nowhere to go and ... it was just purely a confrontation'. Looking back she sees those roles as 'more like characters ... it was a struggle against the character and it seems to me that the struggle in drama is a more interesting one'. She was keen to distinguish these roles of her past from the roles she now takes which do not set up confrontation.

I asked what O'Neill had understood by the girl's comment about her acting at the end of the drama but not at the beginning.

> I think that what she meant was improvising, and I think that she could see that it was less of a scenario ... But I would have thought that I was always more acting at the beginning because I knew my script better than I did later on.

For O'Neill, drama should not be focused on the teacher's role. 'I think teacher-in-role has a quality of presentation or representation of a particular kind of person. In my case it tends to refer to a fairly faceless bureaucratic kind of person'. O'Neill explained that often when she asks children whether they think her role was male or female, they are not really sure, and she reiterated that her roles had a faceless nature.

I asked her what the difference would have been if I had watched the drama as a staged piece with a set and props.

> It would have been very different in that the role of Mrs. Green would have been consistent. I think I would allow myself a level of inconsistency so that I can then become nice ... and then that allows me to either get heavy or anxious or whatever I feel will press their buttons, whatever will be the most effective functionally. Whereas I think if it was to be staged, ... whoever played that part would have to establish a kind of type ... it would have a kind of internal consistency.

She is convinced that 'it is important for the kids to have something to look at so that their minds are taken off themselves'.

O'Neill contrasted her work with that of Jonothan Neelands. She sees his work in role as acting. She articulated two distinctions between her own work and Neelands'. Firstly, he 'becomes' the roles and creates characters. Neelands creates *a* 'distinct individual who has a history and whose history is the meat of the drama'. Secondly, he becomes the focus of the dramas.

> Now he works differently of course and he acts ... he will take on a character and he will become that character. I remember ... he became an African nursing mother. Now in a million years I wouldn't take on a role like that. I wouldn't know how to do it. I wouldn't know how to make it work for me the way he makes those roles work for him ... I couldn't make that kind of a role function in a kind of situation driven way. So he then becomes the subject of the drama and the focus of it ... he does it brilliantly and he's a terrific actor.

O'Neill prefers Bolton's term 'acting behaviour' to 'acting' because the latter 'suggests a formal audience'. But the audience isn't the only issue for her and she frequently returned to the issues of character and economy: 'As our work approaches character, so real acting approaches our work – to participate or whatever doing a much lived down more economical bit of acting'. She identifies herself more closely with Booth's type of work. I suggested that they shared a minimalist approach to roles. She replied, 'Absolutely. The less I can do the better, and a lot of the time I still do too much'. She admires minimalist role. Describing a performance of *Miss Julie*, O'Neill described Christopher Eccleston who took the role of Jean in the following ways: 'he was acting – he was doing too much. I didn't believe his performance'.

> I never think of myself as an actress and I'm not a very good actress ... I don't think I could be the sort of actor who loses himself in the role – I think I would always be thinking functionally ... whereas Jonothan – if he could sort of think himself into that person ... but he presents, he represents it in a way that I don't think I embody those roles like that ... reflecting an elaboration of the text.

> Working with Keith Johnstone, I remember he would say 'Sit next to that person and don't do anything.' It was an impossible task. Then he would say, 'No, you are doing too much. Do less!' Despite the difficulties to achieve this, it is seen as

simple as opposed to complex acting behaviour. My acting behaviour was extremely simple.

When asked to sum up the distinctions a spectator might observe when watching O'Neill and an actor, she explained

> I think an actor would probably have a wider range of movement and gesture at his disposal and indeed vocal possibility because he would have been trained. He would have techniques. He might not use vast gestures unless they were appropriate, but they would have the possibilities of elaboration...

and on role,

> What I'm thinking while I'm doing those fairly limited roles, that fairly limited acting behaviour, means I'm trying to launch the work and I'm trying to launch them in a situation ... and that's what's occupying me rather than any concern with how well I am representing whatever it is.

Analysis of the interview

The interview reveals the thinking that underpins O'Neill's values and assumptions. Three main points emerge that support a distinction between teacher-in-role and actor. I examine her emphases and identify the opposition between teacher-in-role and acting that appears in what she says. O'Neill argues explicitly that teacher-in-role is not acting, but concedes that it may usefully be described as 'acting behaviour'. The table below proposes that there are assumptions about role and acting that have led her to make a distinction between the two, and locates the evidence from the interview. The right hand column provides an extract from the interview to illustrate the point.

O'Neill interview: Differences between Teacher-in-role and Acting

Teacher-in-role is	Acting is	Evidence
Being economical with text	Being elaborative with text	*An actor ... would have the possibilities of elaboration*

Teacher-in-role is	Acting is	Evidence
A representation or presentation	Becoming a character	*Teacher-in-role has a quality of presentation or representation of a particular kind of person.* Re Neelands *he acts – he will take on a character and he will become that character*
Minimalism	Doing too much	*The less I can do, the better, and a lot of the time I still do too much;* Re Eccleston *he was acting. He was doing too much*
Improvising	Working from a script	Girl thought I was not acting at the beginning – *what she meant was improvising... I was more acting at the beginning because I knew my script more than I did later on,* Re actors *they know in advance the full extent of their character's history. They know the character's journey*
Not focus of attention	Focus of attention	*Fairly superficial kind of acting, if it is acting, because it mustn't draw attention.* Distinguishes between her own and Neelands' work *so he becomes the subject of the drama and the focus of it*
Not needing to be consistent during the drama	Consistent in role	*I would allow myself a level of inconsistency ... whereas I think if it*

Teacher-in-role is	Acting is	Evidence
		was staged, whoever played that part would have to establish ... a kind of internal consistency
Remaining outside the role	Embodying or becoming the character	*I want to distance.* Compared with Neelands, who acts, *I don't think I embody those roles like that... The actor, I feel, inhabits a role more fully*
Very simple	Complex	*It is seen as simple as opposed to complex acting behaviour. My acting behaviour was extremely simple*
Having no interest in how well role is represented	Having an interest in how actor is being received by audience	*And that's what's occupying me rather than any concern with how well I'm representing whatever it is...*
Associated with a viewpoint or attitude	Associated with character	*As our work approaches character, so real acting approaches our work*
Working with a participant audience	Working with a formal audience	Likes Bolton's term 'acting behaviour' for role since it is different from '*acting*' which suggests a formal audience
functional	A predetermined journey	*a rather functional thing where you adopt a role. The actor, I feel, inhabits a role more fully, or a character more fully... They know the character's journey'*

This table provides the logic to O'Neill's position. The distinction between teacher-in-role and acting is a rational product of these assumptions about acting and role. The response to the girl's comment provides an interesting example. O'Neill thought that it would have been the other way around, that she was seen as acting at the beginning when she knew a script, but not at the end when she was improvising. Given the assumption that actors work from scripts, and teacher-in-role through improvisation, her logic is straightforward.

Inherent in these assumptions is also a hierarchy: minimalism is clearly desirable, while elaboration is not. The idea of presenting an attitude, rather than a character, is significant. Teacher-in-role need not be concerned with internal commitment to character. This is the business of acting. The notion of acting is the Stanislavskian model. Acting is seen as becoming immersed in a character. O'Neill explains that in *Miss Julie* Eccleston 'was acting. He was doing too much' and she 'didn't believe his performance'. From this it would follow that what is 'too much' is not believable. Minimalism is conceived as authentic. 'Too much' may be taken for over-acting, or perhaps the actor revealing his actor role rather than keeping it concealed. The convention of concealing the effort, skills, and person of the actor is associated with psychological realism. This, too, would connect with O'Neill's notion of 'internal consistency'.

We can identify what O'Neill sees as crucial for role to secure pedagogic success. It is a distanced role requiring no internal psychological process or consistency. What O'Neill admires in acting is consistency, with believable, minimalist signing and naturalist, inner portrayal.

Contextualising the case study

I shall now look at the case study in the light of conceptual distinctions laid out earlier in the theoretical framework in Section One.

Contexts and Audience Relationships – This sample of practice provided a most interesting profile with regard to context and audience relationships. It was carried out not in a classroom but a rehearsal room in the Royal National Theatre. Furthermore, the participants were not present for curriculum learning and their attendance was not compulsory – it was their choice to attend a youth theatre. The participants' expectations were therefore to do drama, and to enjoy it.

These points immediately break down the initial Categorising TIR and Actor Grid: The First Model (Table 1). In my attempt to argue that the distinctions between the two were not so great, I suggested that actors could work with compulsory audiences and outside theatre buildings, just like the teacher-in-role. However, here the gap between teacher-in-role and acting is closed from the other direction. Here the teacher-in-role is at a theatre building, with no pedagogic obligation and voluntary participants who were committed to drama.

While there was no pedagogic obligation, O'Neill clearly had a triple intention which shaped her relationship with the participants. She wished to extend the drama skills of the participants, to give them an enjoyable session (in the interests of the youth theatre), and also to invite them to engage with the subject of genetic engineering. These three intentions do not differentiate O'Neill's practice from that of many actors. Even where there is a non-participant audience, theatre often seeks to extend audience skills in reading theatre through innovative techniques for display or communicating meaning. There is a desire in contemporary theatre to educate audiences to interpret performance that does not follow traditional patterns of communication. Actors in professional theatre are also keen to provide an enjoyable experience, just as O'Neill does. Her desire to raise an issue that interests her is, again, what playwrights and theatre makers do.

In terms of the context and some aspects of the relationship with the young people, this work is closer to that of an actor than of a O'Neill's teacher-in-role (see table page 102).

Functions and Aims – Let us return to the moment in the drama examined earlier from a semiotic perspective. When O'Neill delivered lines in a hesitating, faltering way, she was signalling a personal response by Mrs Green to the situation. She, Mrs Green, was uncomfortable, which is why she hesitated. It took a while for the participants to discover what the problem was. They knew some-

	O'NEILL'S TEACHER-IN-ROLE	USUAL TEACHER-IN-ROLE
Context of drama	a session leader almost unknown to the group in a youth theatre at a theatre rehearsal space	leader is familiar class teacher with school children in a classroom, hall, or drama studio in school
Audience relationship	active participation amongst group	active participation amongst group
Attendance	voluntary	compulsory
Audience expectations	the participants expected to work on theatre skills – the long mirrored room produces particular expectations of theatre activity rather than learning they arrived expecting to enjoy themselves	children expect to learn something about the curriculum or drama some children may expect to enjoy the work
Attitude to participation	all eager to get involved	some children are eager to get involved

thing was wrong, but because Mrs Green was faltering, they didn't know immediately what it was. Clearly, this was a deliberate ploy to inject dramatic tension. In Morgan and Saxton's terms (1987, p7) this is a 'tension of the unknown'. The hesitancy had a clear intention: to make the participants anxious to know what they were not being told. The desire to know makes the delay in the discovery significant. Hence that 'mental excitement', as Bolton describes tension, comes into play. So the hesitancy might be described as functional in this context. The creation of tension was necessary to meet the demands of the art form. Without tension, there would be no interest and therefore no drama. It is an essential component of theatre. This also follows a traditional theatrical structure in which obstacles are set to block off the chance of early resolution to the problems and difficulties posed. O'Neill's hesitating might well have been functional. But an actor's hesitation is also functional.

Mrs Green has a role function, as has the role an actor plays. From Propps' list of role functions, we could place Mrs Green as a helper, even though she was the bearer of bad news. She was an enabler of sorts, the messenger through whom the participants could access information. Alternatively, she could be described as the false helper, since she was in the employ of the organisation perceived as the 'villain'. She might sit more neatly in Aston and Savona's conventional character function of confidante. She was sympathetic to the delegates, and did say that she felt the 'whole thing' had been very badly handled. The confidante functions to provide fictional details required for the drama. It is often the confidante who provides the exposition, setting the scene for the drama to begin. The role of Mrs Green, like all the roles O'Neill now uses, is not protagonist or antagonist but one who serves the protagonist. The participants are thus often thrown into the role of antagonists. In this drama the clones challenge the company's aim to further their research into genetic engineering.

In order to function, O'Neill had to employ skills to signal that Mrs Green was anxious about giving the information. The extract from the interview above exposes some slippage between the notions of the function of the role and of the role player. We can strip the process back to three layers:

1. Functions of the drama

The function of the teacher	to raise awareness about genetic issues
The function of the teacher-in-role	to engineer dramatic contexts through which to explore the issues
The function of the role	to carry out an efficient job at the congress

When Mrs Green hesitates and falters over giving the information, we can identify specific functions at each stage:

2. Functions at a moment in the drama

Breaking up the layers of function in this way enables us to see what is taking place. Firstly, a web of functions is revealed. The teacher has a teaching function, the teacher-in-role a function to

The function of the teacher	to prepare the participants for something they will *disapprove* of
	to avoid confrontation between group and role
The function of the teacher-in-role	to create tension and slow down the action
The function of the role	to ensure the clone delegates will *not get angry or blame her*

create theatre, and the role a function within the narrative. I have suggested that functions are not value-free. Let us suppose that this dramatic structure is adapted by a teacher (Ms X) who is excited by the possibilities of genetic engineering. Her function may be defined as to raise awareness of genetic issues. The functions of teacher-in-role and role could be as for the drama above: engineering dramatic opportunities and carrying out an efficient job at the congress.

1. Functions for Ms X's drama

The function of the teacher	to raise awareness about genetic issues
The function of the teacher-in-role	to engineer dramatic contexts through which to explore the issues
The function of the role	to carry out an efficient job at the congress

But when we move from the general functions to the specific moment in the drama when Mrs Green delivers the news that the congress delegates are all clones, there may be some differences. Ms X, with a positive view of the opportunities afforded by genetic engineering, will prepare the participants for the news differently. The function of the teacher is different. This will in turn have an effect on the function of the teacher-in-role, who could delay by stumbling with excitement, building up the tension as the delegates are framed to anticipate some *exciting* news. It is this moment of preparation for the news of cloning that fulfils the concealed function of teacher. It shapes the way the participants are required to react to the news.

2. Functions at a moment in Ms X's drama

The teacher's function	to prepare the participants for something they will *approve* of
The teacher-in-role's function	to use the art form; creating tension and slowing down action (using two traditional theatrical conventions to achieve both)
The role's function:	to ensure the clone delegates will *be ready for the excitement*

The functions are therefore interconnected and impact on one another. They are shaped by the aims and functions of the teacher. This example compels us to reconsider the use of the word function. It now seems tricky to describe the function of the teacher in value-neutral terms, as 'to raise awareness of genetic issues' is misleading. The O'Neill lesson is raising awareness of the complexities and dangers involved in genetic engineering. (A problem emerges with the genetic engineering. The age of the material brings a fear and concern. The negativity is enhanced by the reference to the newspapers 'getting hold of this.') Ms X's lesson would be raising awareness of the opportunities genetic engineering could bring to human life.

Functions of O'Neill and Ms X

This example serves to remind us that there is no consensus over what should be taught about genetics, and therefore there can be no assumed 'function of teacher'. Clearly, the function of the 'role of teacher' determines the functions of the 'teacher-in-role' and the 'role'. The teacher-in-role and role both serve to provide an artistic logic to the unfolding events, which are planned according to the

	O'Neill	Ms X
The teacher's function	To raise awareness about genetic issues: the complexities and possible problems	To raise awareness about genetic issues: the opportunities genetic engineering could bring to human life

teacher's intentions. In the interview, O'Neill explained that in delivering her role the priority is 'whatever will be the most effective functionally'. This case study exemplifies my earlier proposal that the function of the teacher-in-role cannot be separated from the aims of the teacher. And since the function of the role player is to serve the functions of the overall aims, the teacher-in-role is not doing something significantly different from what an actor often does. The actor functions to fulfil the logic of the play and behaves according to the overall aims and intentions for the production. The case study example challenges a view that the teacher-in-role's function is significantly different from that of the actor.

Skills – While in role, O'Neill shaped the aesthetic experience and structured events for the participants, as is customary in process drama. Appropriate signs were selected and moments made significant and tension created. In order to appear anxious, Mrs. Green had to hesitate, avoid direct eye contact with the participants, and change her oral delivery. She used the skills of signing through voice and gesture, body and facial expression. O'Neill also used her skills in improvisation, particularly spontaneity and narrative skills which are the key skills in Johnstone's improvisation (Johnstone, 1981).

The table opposite identifies skills exhibited by O'Neill. The first list of skills is drawn from those anticipated for the teacher-in-role according to the literature explored in Section One. The second list is taken from the National Council for Drama Training (1999) criteria reproduced earlier.

SKILLS EXHIBITED BY O'NEILL

Skills employed from the sphere of drama in education	structuring the drama like a dramatist signing through voice communicating through gesture improvisation skills i.e. spontaneity, narration skills, selection of significant parts of the oral text as a playwright listening to the participants
	responding to the participants
Skills employed from the sphere of acting	c) create believable character and emotion appropriate to the demands of the text and production
	d) define the objectives of a character and embody and express them within the context of a production
	f) work sensitively with other actors in rehearsal and performance
	g) show evidence in performance of creative imagination, emotion, thought, concentration and energy
	h) develop an effective working process and the ability to monitor and evaluate its application
	j) prepare and sustain the quality of concentration necessary for each performance
	m) communicate to an audience with expression, emotion and spontaneity
	n) adjust to the demands of different venues and media
	o) adjust to the nature and reaction of different audiences
	t) create and sustain an improvised rehearsal or performance with discipline and spontaneity

The National Council for Drama Training criteria note that skills in characterisation are important for acting. The characteristics I noted of Mrs Green's presentation were:

anxiety, communicated through her gesture and hesitation

defensiveness, because she refused to take any responsibility

secrecy, because it became obvious that she knew more than she told the participants

manipulation in the way that she made the media a threat, to force the participants to keep quiet

subservience, since she followed what her superiors instructed even when she was not entirely sure that this was the right course of action

While these were clearly designed to have a particular effect upon the participants, it does not negate the features as characteristics that were skilfully revealed through the drama, through what are, I suggest, O'Neill's acting skills.

Approaches – In this drama it is difficult to distinguish between the character and the functions of the character, as Aston and Savona suggest (1991, p46). We see Mrs Green as an anxious character only because the role had to function to stall information so as to build tension and ensure that the teacher's role could not be blamed. O'Neill was determined that her role should not be the focus of the drama: as long as Mrs Green was not herself the perpetrator of any unpleasantness, she could not be blamed for it. This avoided confrontation and maintained the focus on the issue rather than on Mrs. Green herself.

In O'Neill's view, Mrs Green was not a character. O'Neill did not 'become immersed' or remain 'consistent', but there were traits that identified Mrs Green and I would argue that she was not inconsistent. She was calm when all was well at the beginning, and unsettled when she discovered she had a nasty job to do. This is understandable and recognisable human behaviour. There was, as we have seen, some personality revealed through her response, although it was obviously a construct, purely to serve the drama, just as it would be in any piece of theatre. O'Neill wants 'to distance' through her role. Her distance was evident at points in the drama when the artifice of the fictitious event was exposed, for instance she chose not to make any gestures to distinguish Mrs Green from the teacher out of role. The lack of physical or special changes exposes the pretence. Another example is apparent early in the drama, whe the famous people were invited to introduce themselves. Obviously this was a dramatic ploy, since in real life famous people would probably have known or known of each other. It exposes the duality of theatre.

This distance through the role contrasts with the approach Ibsen would have expected of an actor playing Nora Helmer. He wanted the character to draw audiences in. He claimed to know all about his characters (Ibsen, 1993). He understood more than was ever revealed of his characters in his plays, and hence a psychological integrity was required to play her as he intended. O'Neill does not need to know the sides of Mrs Green that are irrelevant to her social role as a congress convenor. This does not mean that she is not engaged in acting behaviour, merely that she is not engaged in the type of acting sought by Ibsen.

O'Neill is uncomfortable with the notion of her roles being defined as characters, since she associates characters with acting. Acting a character requires an emotional engagement for the portrayal. This is not a position, however, held by theorists such as Hyman, who questions the term 'character' as being a 'dangerous word because it implies a coherence, a consistency and an individuality, which may not be there' (1977, p50). So there is an alternative view that 'character' and 'consistency' may not necessarily be so closely associated one with the other. Simon Callow makes the point that not all acting parts require emotional engagement. O'Neill's role had particular requirements, as did Callow's roles in *Fanshen* and *Mary Barnes*. Although characteristics were revealed, no attempt was made to construct a fully developed character. Both internal and external approaches, as identified earlier, were non-existent at the beginning of the drama, but as we have seen, external signs developed with the dramatic tension. Mrs Green operated through a conventionalised understanding of role, when a character is 'a function of action and of the thematic and ideological underpinnings of action' (Aston and Savona, p34). Hence the character traits are entirely connected with the action.

Comment

The case study has, through both session and interview, yielded insight into how O'Neill's drama operates. The semiotic analysis leads to the conclusion that O'Neill is acting when she works in role. However, the analysis of the interview reveals the logic of O'Neill's position: that acting is something very different. This view might well have some logical consistency based upon her assumptions, which are largely those examined in Section One as dominant in the literature of drama in education. However, it is somewhat less convincing when viewed from a position informed by theories of acting. What O'Neill did falls into Kirby's 'simple acting' category since not many acting dimensions are used, but an impersonation took place.

The sample of O'Neill's practice has enabled close connections to be made between teacher-in-role and acting in all four areas examined. The context of the session was striking for being in a theatre rehearsal room. The role can be seen to function in the same way as a role in theatre, while O'Neill revealed many skills that can be identified as acting skills. The approach of creating a distance between the role and the role player is easily identified in theatrical terms, just as the relationship between character and action.

I would argue that as a result of the analysis of both assumptions and practice through the theoretical lens, the distinction between teacher-in-role and actor looks fragile.

10

Case study – JOHN O'TOOLE

O'Toole taught for three years in rural Cambridgeshire before moving to the North East. He worked for six years at Gateshead's Highfield Comprehensive School with David Davis, Mike Fleming and Geoff Gillham, all of whom later became notable figures in the field of drama in education. He and others from the Durham MA group set up a part-time theatre in education company, 'South Tyneside TIE', developing projects with 'low-key fully integrated participation' (2001). O'Tool, currently Associate Professor at Griffith University, Queensland, O'Toole is probably best known for his book entitled *The Process of Drama* (1992). This was the culmination of his Ph.D thesis, which he chose to undertake in a theatre department rather than an education department. O'Toole is credited for his theoretical framing of drama practice in theatre terms in this book.

Like O'Neill, he first came upon teacher-in-role on Bolton's course in Durham in 1968 and watched him and Heathcote using it. He was 'blown away by its possibilities'. His work in theatre in education influenced his classroom practice and it is to this that he ascribes his respect for theatricality in teacher-in-role. He has nonetheless stressed to teachers new to drama that teacher-in-role 'did not have to be showy, nor did you have to be an actor.' 'The relationship between the two words in the phrase 'actor-teacher' was one of the most interesting features' (*ibid*) to O'Toole when he wrote his first book, *Theatre in Education* (1977).

O'Toole claims to have been influenced by the practice of many teachers and students he has observed. 'It was really fascinating to watch and contrast Dorothy, so big and theatrical, yet beautifully anchored and down-to-earth, and Gavin, so absolutely minimal, but the kids were just as focused and rapt' (2001).

He sees himself as 'one of the mappers, advocates and collaborative consolidators' of the field. He is 'actually very proud of the development of drama in education in Australia, in which [he has] certainly played a part, in pushing and wheedling, in laying the ground intellectually and practically, and in sustaining a collaborative ethos.' He feels that 'in their own way both *Dramawise* (1988) and *The Process of Drama* (1992) maybe have helped to define and clarify the terminology, the concepts and the territory.' He has sought to 'analyse what 'process' actually means, what the elements of drama are, and how the dramatic art form intersects or interacts with learning' (*ibid*).

CONTEXT OF OBSERVATION

When	1 September, 1999
With whom	Second year education students who had all opted for a programme in drama.
Duration	2 hours.
Where	Griffith University, Brisbane, Queensland, Australia
Participants	18 young people aged between 19 and 23 who did not know each other well
Gender/ethnic mix	Majority of women, predominantly white Australian. One Chinese student spoke English as her second language.
Space	A purpose built drama studio that was comfortable, carpeted, spacious yet intimate. There was raked seating and a stage opposite, with a broad working space between.
Experience	Most had had only a brief introduction to drama in education.
Knowledge of leader	They had not worked with O'Toole before.

Narrative account of session

This drama was constructed to explore the origin of the Australian song, *Waltzing Matilda*. It was being taught to student teachers who could engage in it at their own level but see it also as suitable for their classrooms. The aim was to explore two versions of the song and to, in O'Toole's words, 'find out what it actually means and why it means that'.

O'Toole asked the group to join with him in singing the song. He then deliberately confused them by singing an unfamiliar version. Then they all sang the familiar version together.

Stage 1

The fictional context opened in the future, in 3005. O'Toole was in role as the congress convenor. He explained to the assembled linguistic experts that since they had specialised in the dead language of 'Ing-glish' they might be able to make sense of an exciting discovery. A relic had been discovered in a country that once existed called, 'Aw stray-lea'. They all knew that very few relics had ever been retrieved since the obliteration. The discovery was bits of writing. It would be very difficult to work out what it all meant, but those at the congress were invited to work in groups to see if they could hazard some informed guesses about the meanings of the strange words. It was generally thought that 'Matilda' must have been a god, and that 'billy' was probably the name given to a son and that people sacrificed their sons for the god.

Stage 2

The convenor offered the linguists the opportunity to make the most of new technology. Some human remains had been dug up from the same period, around 1890. The remains had been genetically injected so that the human, Jack McCann, was reconstructed. The linguists were invited to see if talking to him could help them to make sense of the fragments they had found.

O'Toole, in role as the swagman, explained terms such as 'swagger', and clarified elements of the past through his 'magic lantern' – an overhead projector showing images of coolibah trees, waterholes and billabongs.

Stage 3

As teacher, O'Toole explained that history always fails to pass down all the facts. He likened it to a tree. There are a certain number of leaves, but when they fall they scatter so that bits of evidence have to be gathered from here and there. As he said this, he threw some pieces of card into the air and invited the groups to gather them up. Each card was identified as A, B or C. Once gathered together, the cards of each letter told a different story of the derivation of *Waltzing Matilda*. Each group shared the information they had learnt from the cards:

There was a depression in 1891-94. Wages had been reduced and shearers went on strike for five years. There had been an arson attack on a barn. It was obviously assumed to be the work of the embittered shearers and swaggers. It was then that Mr. Banjo Patterson had written the song.

Stage 4

The group was split into two. One half were the 'inlaws'. These people saw themselves as respectable rich landowners and shop owners supportive of the status quo. The other half were the 'outlaws', who were against the way things were being run. They included the impoverished, striking shearers and swaggers with no jobs. Both groups created images to depict their contexts.

Then a scene was set in a hotel bar. It was a very special night because a singer was coming to sing a brand new song, which they would all love. A visiting 'Brit', Sir Herbert Ramsey, would sing Banjo Patterson's song. He sang in an upper class English voice and took a collection at the end for the restoration of a barn which had been burnt down. The 'outlaws' were rather rowdy and not too inclined to contribute to the collection.

O'Toole stopped the drama to explain that this related how the song may have first been sung. However, there is another version. They reran the scene, but this time O'Toole took the role of Mr. One Eye'd McCarthy, an Irish immigrant who wore a leather hat and an eye patch. He sang a slightly different tune – the one O'Toole began the session with. I noticed that some of the 'in-laws' did not join in when he sang this time since he clearly identified himself with the 'outlaws'.

Stage 5

O'Toole's narration was about a theatre festival being organised because the hotel had had such a successful evening. Groups were invited to create twenty seconds worth of plays which both groups of people might have produced. The 'outlaws' depicted the swaggers starving and forced into sheep stealing whilst the 'inlaws' demonstrated the injustice of working hard to keep the sheep alive, only to have them stolen.

O'Toole's narration then moved the context forward to 1996, when there were celebrations to mark the song's centenary. All were asked to take the roles of 16 year old school pupils who represented the descendants of those in the drama they had just created. Each was asked to imagine that they had just seen the short plays as part of the centenary celebrations. They were each required to produce two sentences: one to position their attitude to the law, and one to explain why one of the plays had made an impact on them.

O'Toole explained that during the three years of the Boer War, soldiers had sung the same song. The soldiers would have come from a mix of 'in' and 'out' law backgrounds, but they all sang the same song. He imagined that the song could be sung from both positions.

Semiotic analysis of session

Below I apply my generalised semiotic framework to each role played by O'Toole, including that of the narrator, in the same way as with O'Neill's drama.

Semiotic analysis: personas in stages 1,2,3,4 and 5

The table on page 116/117 highlights the changes that were distinguishable between O'Toole as teacher, congress convenor and the three roles and as narrator. The metonymic accessories (costumes, properties, etc) changed for each named role and worked together with the role player to communicate meaning. The semiotic analysis indicates significant change between O'Toole as teacher and as narrator, which is interesting since the narrator was not strictly identified as a role. There was no costume change, just a shift in language register, gesture and kinesic and proxemic features. This might usefully be identified as the type of activity that

Transmitters	Teacher	Congress convenor	Jack McCann	One Eye'd McCarthy	Sir Herbert	Narrator
Oral text	Straight-forward, clear language, semi-formal register	Same, but more specialist linguistic neologisms and deliberate mispronunciation	Slang, language of the working context and region Short exclamations, eg. 'I ask ya'.	Slang, familiar, down to earth language, e.g. 'eh, cobbers'	Precise choice of language, formal and articulate	Poetic, formal, elaborate, figurative language e.g.'leaves of history'
Para-linguistic features	Moderate volume, regular pace, moderate pitch	Same, but slightly louder	Thick, rough Australian accent. volume, with words often spoken through laughter	Irish accent. Regular pace, moderate volume, with varied pitch	Upper class English accent. Low volume, even pace and pitch	Theatrical significance given to words through pace, rhythm and enunciation, and contrast in volume
Kinesic factors	Minimal gesture, standing still with some minor hand movement	Same, but some very deliberate minor hand gestures	Angular gait with protruding elbows and knees	Jerky, but confident gestures	Mannered gestures, head tilting upwards, and eyes that looked down on some of those he spoke to	Deliberate, consciously theatrical gestures

Transmitters	Teacher	Congress convenor	Jack McCann	One Eye'd McCarthy	Sir Herbert	Narrator
Proxemic relations	In front of participants, at close proximity	Same	Sitting in his own space on a stool in front of the linguists with a table between him and the participants	Sitting on a stool in front of the inlaws and outlaws, with no barrier between them	Sitting on a stool in front of the inlaws and outlaws, with no barrier between them	Moving in among the participants
Vestiment-ary codes	Trousers and shirt	Same	Same with a waistcoat	Same with an eye patch	Same with a wide brimmed hat	Same
Properties	None	None	A overhead projector that represented a hologram bringing images from the past	Guitar	Guitar	Cards with historical information

Kirby calls 'performance' since there is a consciousness of audience, yet no pretence to be anyone else. The roles of McCann, One Ey'd McCarthy and Sir Herbert are different, as they are feigned identities.

The moment selected for analysis appears in Stage 4 of the drama. Sir Herbert is addressing the two groups of audience in a crowded bar. The 'outlaws' are on his left, joining in the singing in a very rowdy way. The subdued 'inlaws' are on his right. Sir Herbert's pause during his song is the moment for semiotic examination.

Semiotic analysis: a moment of drama

To further contextualise this moment it is worth adding that when Sir Herbert had finished singing the song, he invited donations for the poor 'inlaws' who had had a barn burned down by the striking shearers.

Here again the semiotic approach provides useful insights. The hand gestures operated more powerfully in the communication process than the words themselves. The signing of the teacher-in-role was crucial to incite the required irritation from the 'outlaws'. As a result of this semiotic analysis, I have watched and re-watched the video to accurately describe the two hand positions at the beginning and end of this moment of dramatic action. The contrast between them is striking. The first is harsh, sharp, flat and dominating, while the second is offering, empowering and respectful. The oral text, whether planned or improvised, is relevant, with its use of 'gentle' and 'good' but its relevance is only made significant by additional considerations. '...the conversational use of spoken language cannot properly be understood unless paralinguistic elements are taken into account' (Abercrombie, 1968, p55).

The interview

I asked O'Toole how he would describe what he does in role.

> Whatever I'm trying to construct, the first thing I obviously do is identify the purpose of the role and along with that try to identify a status level that will not only facilitate the purpose but allow my intervention actually to be quite minimum. So my first concerns are to find the purpose and the status of the

Encoding of meaning				Decoding of meaning		
Source of information	Oral text	Paralinguistic register	Kinesic factors	Meaning	Intention	Desired audience reaction
O'Toole	'We might just sing it a little more gently to allow these good folk here to give it a whirl.'	Smooth even rhythm, slow delivery, with no pauses and no hesitation. Loud and steady with clear enunciation.	Right hand raised across the body like a 'stop' signal to the 'outlaws', then the arm moves to the right, lowering as it does so with the palm turning upwards. The sharp stiffness of the first gesture shifts to a looser position where the fingers are no longer stiff and straight, but slightly curved.	I am on the side of the 'inlaws'. I wish to give them voice and respect. Your voice is not wanted.	To increase the tensions between the two groups.To demonstrate the privileged 'inlaws' over the 'outlaws'.	Be drawn to consider the social difference and thus the extreme difference in power and life styles.

role. I often like to play low status roles so that even if I am playing a high status role, I try and find a way in for the kids to have some power over me. I think in a way there was a bit of that in all of them.

O'Toole explained the purpose of the roles he played and what distinguished them from one another. The range covered 'shadowy' roles, caricatures and theatrical teacher narration.

He described the congress convenor as a 'low key role', 'it was an unnamed role'. He distinguishes between how he would have been perceived as a teacher and in this first role.

I used a change of signalling, I think. I tried to indicate that I was somebody else in what I was saying; I was immediately enrolling them as somebody else. 'Ladies and Gentlemen', I mean, lecturers don't usually say 'Ladies and Gentleman' – well, I don't.

I hope that I was laying a trail of language that was sufficiently interesting and appropriate to the task. So the way I think the performance element was, was mostly in the language and least in the gesture. I was certainly using a special language relating to the historical position of the linguists, and I also started laying trails, dropping hints for use of the word 'English' to be used later.

O'Toole introduced the word 'performance' to describe this role. Given the task was to set up a fictional context, he explained,

I think I deliberately used very very minimal role signals, particularly physical ones; I didn't try and come on as an interesting character in himself. It was important they focused on the task, not the character.

I asked him if he thought that the congress convenor was a 'character' or a 'role'.

Well in the sense that it was a fictional person, he was a character in the fictionalised set up of linguist in the future, and this was the congress convenor inviting them. So in the standard sense of the word 'character', I was taking on the role of that fictional character.

O'Toole also identified a clear function for Jack McCann, his second role. It was 'to give them opportunity to get the history right again... an information giving role'. Continually referring to the status of teacher roles, O'Toole saw this role as 'low status'. 'He (McCann) had knowledge, they had power.' Unlike the congress convenor role, Jack had required extensive research.

> I had to know enough about sheep to play authentically an old cow cockier or a sheep grazier because there might have been students who knew a great deal about grazing, so in that sense it was a tightly constructed fictional character. I actually put on quite a strong accent which I hoped was a real Australian accent or a believable Australian accent. I also used a lot of slang.

He added, 'I did take care making him a person this time'.

Sir Herbert and One Eye'd McCarthy were in O'Toole's mind 'mirror images of each other', used to provide 'a way to look at the deep social divisions that existed'. He suggests that they were 'very much simple stereotype caricatures'.

> They were meant to be a pompous upper class pom, and a jolly larakin drover. McCarthy and Sir Herbert were both real people and so that was where, I guess, I deliberately simplify and falsify history. Probably Sir Herbert was a very nice chap and not an absolute pompous twit. One Ey'd McCarthy might have been a rogue and a liar, I don't know.

The 'role' we both found most interesting to discuss was the teacher/narrator role. When O'Toole narrated details about history and evidence, 'the leaves of history' part of his narration, he was obviously not in role in one sense, and yet he was clearly not purely teacher in another.

> When I told them the story of how the song became famous, taking the teacher's real life role or not, of the storyteller, I was taking a stand or a position which was not being ordinary life; a quite different voice. I was adopting a position, a narrator position and performing it quite hard.

This was the moment when O'Toole threw pieces of paper into the air to make a point emphatically. I suggested that there may have been more theatricality in this non-role moment than in the clearly defined role of the congress convenor.

Yes, that's right. There was a skeletal persona in the convenor in terms of how I performed it, or lived it. An interesting distinction: I was more in the real world, in the real context as the narrator. I suspect I probably used my voice and gesture more theatrically because I was trying to highlight theatrically a moment of real life if you like, whereas as the convenor I was trying to minimalise a moment of dramatic action and characterisation. I was trying to set up a physical moment of theatre, an image. I had to minimalise the role because I didn't want the students to concentrate on me. I wanted them to concentrate on the bits of paper and similarly when I was asking questions I wanted them to concentrate on the story they had concocted.

He went on to explain that this narrator role

was a role that had one foot in the normal use of the word role that we use as the persona for the teacher demonstrating in the public action with the children in their classroom, and the other foot was in the dramatic context and I was hoping to further the dramatic context with it. I think that was only one step behind my first role of the convenor.

When I asked about role, character and acting, O'Toole talked of a continuum along which one may chart types of role/acting behaviour.

In a way this is the continuum I am talking about and in a way the words role and character when they are put as polarities aren't necessarily helpful, though they can be useful. So I would say those first two I guess were roles in a primitive sense, the future congress convenor was a character but he had a clear sort of employment function as a congress convenor. I mean, there was almost a prototype character, an outline sketchpad character.

I wondered whether an emotional engagement with the role has any significance.

> As the storyteller [narrator/teacher] I was actually getting right into telling the story of Waltzing Matilda and the First World War and how I got right into it! There was certainly an emotional engagement there. There was the least emotional engagement, I guess, as the convenor when, as I say, my aim was to make it minimal and I was almost not able to be there.

Analysis of interview

In considering the assumptions and conceptualisations that underpin O'Toole's thinking, it is worth noting that O'Toole told me that it was his theatre in education experience that had given him an enduring 'respect for theatricality in teacher-in-role'. Details from the interview and examples from the session are systematically laid out below in a table that demonstrates my interpretation of what O'Toole believes about role. These views appear in the left hand column, any qualifications to these views in the middle column, and the evidence in the right.

O'Toole interview: Views on teacher-in-role

View on role	Qualifying point/s	Evidence
Can use costume	does not have to do so	congress convenor had no costume, but other three roles had waistcoat, eye patch or hat
Can use properties	does not have to do so	congress convenor used no properties, but McCann had a magic lantern and the other two had guitars.
	teacher can use resources (properties) out of role	teacher used information cards

View on role	Qualifying point/s	Evidence
Can use space theatrically – designating space and using proxemics: shape and spatial organisation	does not have to do so	congress convenor used the space conventionally as a teacher uses it. McCann took his own space apart from the participants
	teacher can use space theatrically out of role	teacher/narrator moved between participants when throwing cards
Can be a caricature	role does not have to be caricature	*unlike Jack McCann, both Sir Herbert and One Ey'd McCarthy were very much simple stereotype caricatures.*
Can involve emotional commitment	teaching can involve emotional commitment, too	*as the story teller [narrator/teacher] I was actually getting right into telling the story of Waltzing Matilda and the First World War and how I got right into it! There was certainly an emotional engagement there.*
	role does not have to do so	*There was the least emotional engagement, I guess, as the convenor*
Played in a minimalist way it does not involve emotion		*there was least emotional engagement, I guess, as the convenor when as I say, my aim was to make it minimal and I was*

View on role	Qualifying point/s	Evidence
Can be a character	there are different degrees of characterisation	*the words role and character when they are put as polarities aren't necessarily helpful... those first two were roles in a primitive sense. The future congress convenor was a character but he had a clear sort of employment function as a congress convenor. I mean, there was almost a prototype character, an outline sketchpad character.*
Should not draw attention		*It was important they focused on the task, not the character* (re convenor)

The table reveals a very broad view of what teacher-in-role can be and a view that while teacher-in-role can be highly theatrical, so too, can teaching out of role.

Role is not given strict parameters. Nothing appears to be excluded, at least as a possibility. The theatricality out of role was developed in order 'to emphasise a point', and yet limited in role to prevent the role becoming 'the focus of attention'.

The role of the congress convenor was articulated as minimally played, just as O'Neill's congress convenor. Yet other roles were not specifically articulated as minimal. This aspect of the differences between the roles was not discussed. The interview included familiar discourse about teacher-in-role, creating the same conceptualisations as O'Neill, such as

- 'adopting a position'
- 'low key role'
- the importance of the participants 'being focused on the task, not the character
- 'minimalist' role taking
- 'behind the scenes sort of role'

O'Toole referred to these familiar ideas in relation to the congress convenor but not to Jack McCann, One Ey'd McCarthy or Sir Herbert. They do not fit the discourse he continues to use, yet he provides no alternative notion of role in relation to these particular roles. From this interview it is clear that O'Toole articulates what has been unquestioned by the field in general, yet does not respond to the fact that this discourse does not seem to describe many of the roles he takes. He is, however, fully aware of the theatricality of his work, as we have seen, and has a much broader notion of teacher-in-role than he actually articulates in these familiar adages.

O'Toole explained the teacher as narrator who tells about the 'leaves of history' as 'a stand or position which was not being ordinary life, a quite different voice. I was adopting a position, a narrator position and performing it quite hard'. He used the terms 'performing' and 'character' freely when referring to the roles he had played. He did not, however, speak about 'acting'. He argued against a distinction between role and character by putting them onto one continuum. The congress convenor, therefore, would be closer to the 'role' end of the continuum, and Sir Herbert towards 'character' at the other. But it becomes clear that he has a different understanding of 'character' than O'Neill does. The convenor was a 'kind of prototype character, an outline, sketch pad character', but he does not assume that any inner engagement or elaboration is required. Although he refers to 'prototype' characters, his theory leans towards the givens of drama in education.

Contextualising the case study

This case study too is examined according to conceptual distinctions laid out in the theoretical framework in Section One.

Context and Audience Relationships – The context for this sample of practice was, again, not the most common for drama in education. The space was a purpose built drama studio at a university and the participants were young adults who had opted for a course in drama in education in their teacher-training programme. Like a traditional theatre audience, attendance was voluntary, but unlike it, their expectations were to learn. In this context, to learn how they could use drama as teachers in the classroom. Again, the original Categorising TIR and Actor Grid: The First Model on page 5 is disrupted in that the drama studio venue and the voluntary participants would be more likely to appear in the actor's column than the teacher-in-role's. Given, too, that working with active participants might be as much a part of an actor's work as a teacher-in-role's, there is little to substantiate a distinction between O'Toole's teacher-in-role and acting with regards to context and audience relationships.

Functions and Aims – Interestingly, when I asked O'Toole what he does when taking a role, he, like O'Neill, talked about aims and functions. The dominant discourse, as we have seen, identifies drama education as a way to seek and discover 'truth' and 'meaning'. However, O'Toole has argued that drama practice has been too 'comfortable' and suggested that alternative positions should be 'played with'; that those with which we do not agree should not be excluded from the classroom (conference paper, 2001). Yet O'Toole reproduces the familiar 'truth' rationale in the interview, even though the drama purports to be offering different possibilities concerning the origins of *Waltzing Matilda*. These complexities and possibilities are now examined step by step

When introducing it to student teachers, O'Toole explained that the drama was to explore 'what the song actually means and why it was written'. The use of 'actually' suggests that there have been some misunderstandings, but there is an 'actual' meaning that will be discovered through the drama. Given this aim, it is easy to see how the role of Jack McCann fulfils his purpose to provide information that will lead towards an understanding of what the song *actually means*. McCann is able to explain what some of the terms mean and explain the context of sheep swaggers when the song was written. His role function would, therefore, be identified by Propp as the helper.

1. Functions of the drama – McCann

The function of the teacher	to explore 'what the song actually means and why it was written',
The function of the teacher-in-role	'to give them opportunity to get the history right again; an information giving role'.
The function of the role	to tell the linguists about his life on the land.

Strikingly, this table highlights the function of the 'role of teacher' determining the functions of the 'teacher-in-role' and therefore the 'role' exactly like the function table in the O'Neill case study.

Turning to Sir Herbert and the moment analysed earlier, we can also identify specific functions. This role is used to approach the second part of the aim – the social divisions.

2. Functions at a moment in the drama – Sir Herbert

The function of the teacher	to highlight the social divisions between the two groups
The function of the teacher-in-role	to create tension between the groups and provoke a reaction from the group in role as 'outlaws' (within the logic of the drama)
The function of the role	to entertain his audience and ensure the 'inlaw' group, with whom he identifies, enjoy themselves, have a role in the event, and are not overwhelmed by the 'outlaws'

Again, a web of functions is revealed. The teacher has a teaching function, the teacher-in-role a function to create dramatic tension, and the role to function within the narrative. The function within the narrative is again an inevitable product of the teacher's aims. Sir Hubert functioned to highlight social divisions and draw the outlaws' attention to them.

The scene with Sir Herbert singing in the hotel was then re-run with O'Toole offering a different possibility for the first ever rendition of the song. McCarthy, on the side of the 'outlaws', made his allegiance equally clear. So there are two possible versions of events. This presentation of different possibilities appears to support the view that O'Toole articulates about the need for drama to play with a range of viewpoints and not just the 'politically correct' ones (*ibid*). It promotes a view of alternatives, a breaking down of grand narratives. It goes against the view of finding an 'actual' meaning by offering two histories. This drama at first appears to be a clear attempt to break down the view of a single version of the truth.

However, it does not offer equal credibility to each version. The lesson is taught from a position that is sympathetic to the 'outlaws'.

> Sir Herbert was meant to be a pompous upper class pom, and One Ey'd McCarthy was meant to be a jolly larakin drover ... [they] were both real people and so I guess I deliberately simplified and falsified history. Probably Sir Herbert was a very nice chap and not at all an absolute pompous twit. One Ey'd McCarthy might have been a rogue and a liar, I don't know, but ... it was grounded in truth so we could take liberties with it to find out the truth.

Who will believe a pompous twit? We are presented with a radical perspective, due to a desire to reveal the social differences with a particular political bias. Sir Herbert might have been a 'nice chap', but had he been a nice chap in the drama, criticism of the ruling class would not have been so evident. As a 'pompous twit', he contrasted with the affable, good-humoured jolly drover, McCarthy. The power differential works against the likeable character, so the participants see the situation as unjust. Creating Herbert as pompous guarantees a negative reaction from the participants. So since the drama presents a rich man as the buffoon and the worker as the hero, the two positions are not really presented equally, and the drama is intrinsically involved in values. A liberal, leftist perspective is privileged as 'actual'. However much one may sympathise, it cannot be portrayed as universal truth. For example, the indigenous aboriginal perspective is totally invisible and would, I imagine, offer a different critical lens through which to view the history of Australia's national anthem.

Whether O'Toole is offering us one meaning or several possible versions, in foregrounding alternative versions of reality he is clearly grappling with an important issue for the field which deserves attention. In this thesis, however, it is not my focus, except for the implication it provides. This examination suggests that despite O'Toole's particular position on the dangers of proposing one version of reality in drama as 'the truth', he still uses language that contradicts this intention. This parallels another apparent contradiction between intention and articulation. O'Toole uses the familiar discourse about role as minimal and the teacher-in-role needing to avoid attention seeking, yet constructs roles that are not minimalist and that demand attention. His current discourse clearly contains residual elements from the traditionally dominant discourse of drama in education.

This examination of function also reinforces my argument that there is no one function of teacher-in-role that is divorced from the aims of the lesson, and therefore, no teacher-in-role function that is any more value-free than the aims.

Skills

The skills required to perform O'Toole's different roles were not the same as those needed by O'Neill, though there are some commonalities. O'Toole changed his voice and altered his language for the roles and he manipulated the rhythm of the drama. Contrasts between volume, dramatic pace and accent and costume were much in evidence. It was impossible not to be struck by the theatrical choices being made and the theatrical skills being exhibited at every stage. O'Toole probably employed a broader range of skills when he was in the three named roles than when he was the congress convenor. O'Toole described the two singing roles as 'high level – I wanted to be listened to'. The accents may have taxed many a drama teacher because there were so many: Australian, upper class English, and Irish. There was also skilful use of mannerisms to signify the role types. Even posture spoke of who the named character was. Many of these skills, such as selecting specific posture and using accents, are not noted in the literature as required or recommended for a teacher-in-role, but are obviously associated with acting. Those recommended in the literature of the field of drama in education are the same as those identified in O'Neill's work. Here the list of acting skills is much longer.

SKILLS EXHIBITED BY O'TOOLE

Skills employed from the the sphere of drama in education	structuring the drama like a dramatist signing through voice communicating through gesture improvisation skills i.e. spontaneity, narration skills, selection of significant parts of the oral text as a playwright listening to the participants responding to the participants
Skills employed from the sphere of acting	a) develop and play a character in rehearsals and performances and sustain it before an audience within a framework of a production as directed b) show evidence of the skills of characterisation c) create believable character and emotion appropriate to the demands of the text and production d) define the objectives of a character and embody and express them within the context of a production e) make full use of individuality of performance f) work sensitively with other actors in rehearsal and performance

g)   show evidence within performance of creative imagination, emotion, thought, concentration and energy

h) develop an effective working process and the ability to monitor and evaluate its application

i) draw upon and make use of personal experience and observation to assist in the creation of a role

j) prepare and sustain the quality of concentration necessary for each performance

k) combine acting with singing and/or dancing and other appropriate skills

l) use [make-up] costumes and props effectively to develop performance

m) communicate to an audience with expression, emotion and spontaneity

n) adjust to the demands of different venues and media

o) adjust to the nature and reaction of different audiences

p) read and interpret texts with accuracy and confidence [Waltzing Matilda]

q) identify style and form of writing in order to reveal and express these elements within a performance

r) use textual analysis, research and observation in the development of a role

t) create and sustain an improvised rehearsal or performance with discipline and spontaneity

The only criteria from the acting list that were not exhibited by O'Toole are

s) study text, in both prose and verse, and make full use of the structures and phrasing in order to reveal character, intention and the development of a story.

u) show evidence of ability to devise and where appropriate, to direct, performance material from research and observation.

Thus it is difficult to conceive of what O'Toole did in role as anything other than acting.

Approaches

O'Toole's external approaches to role were far more explicit than O'Neill's, using costumes, voice changes, accents, props and large gestures. O'Toole's caricatures of McCarthy and Sir Herbert are similar to those of the commedia character types. These characters are stock characters who make the audience laugh because they are familiar. 'Each character is the representative of a social class which, by the act of theatre, becomes the magical incarnation of all its class' (Boso, 1980, p9). O'Toole used McCarthy and Herbert to 'look at the deep social divisions' and they become 'the magical incarnation of all [their] classes'. The students at once recognised the upper class Sir Hubert as a pretentious idiot, and would have known the character type. Equally, they would recognise the daring and cheeky, carefree McCarthy, who was working for the best he could get, from the position of the under-dog.

Sir Herbert resembles the old man Pantalone from Commedia dell'arte. He is rich and enjoys high status. He is keen to hold onto his wealth and position

> Inherent in this attempt to hold on to an old order is Pantelone's influence as a stabilising figure, limiting the world view of Commedia, and thus enabling it to endure whilst bursting at the seams as the young (the Lovers) and the dispossessed (the zanni) eternally attempt a take-over. (Rudlin, 1994, p92)

Sir Herbert wishes to maintain the status quo while the dispossessed sheep shearers and especially McCarthy, attempt to dislodge it. McCarthy in some respects resembles Arlecchino, 'distinguished from the zanni by having enough intelligence to hatch schemes' (*ibid* p79).

Another obvious connection is to Brecht. Like Brecht's roles, Sir Herbert and McCarthy could not be analysed psychologically; their characteristics are 'inscribed by their *social actions*' (Counsell, 1996, p86). The semiotic analysis of a moment of the drama revealed a moment that fulfils Brecht's concept of *gestus*. This, Counsell explains, 'entailed finding performance signs capable of indicating social positions and relationships ... in the *gesture*, the actor's action is encoded the gist of the social relationships in which the actors is enmeshed' (*ibid*). Sir Herbert's hand gestures, analysed earlier, expose the social relationships he had to both the 'inlaws' and 'outlaws'.

There is a complexity here, however. One Eye'd McCarthy and Sir Herbert were both roles of performers in performance. O'Toole, the role player, had to 'perform' in both roles with an awareness of his audience. The audience were students at one level and 'inlaws' and 'outlaws' at the fictional level. It could be argued that O'Toole had to use performance and his acting skills to play the roles of performers. I include his musical skills as performance. At these points, when the roles were performers, there was a complex web of dramatic action. The roles (McCarthy and Sir Herbert) were performing in direct presentational mode, being open about their act in front of their audiences. States would identify these two as working in expressive modes since they were singers displaying their artistry to their audience. At the same time, we must consider the role player, O'Toole. He was inviting the students to become part of the fictional hotel bar, and to join the scene by responding to the two performers. He broke 'down the distance between actor and audience ... to give the spectator something more than a passive role in the theatre exchange' (States, 1996, p29). This is a collaborative model of theatre. Here again, we find the practice of teacher-in-role is clearly described through theatrical theory.

These flamboyant roles of Sir Hubert and McCarthy can be contrasted with the approach taken by O'Toole when he plays the congress convenor who is setting the context and giving information to aid the participants' understanding. In this it corresponds to Brecht's 'The Announcer' in *The Resistable Rise of Arturo Ui* (1981, [1941] and the storyteller in African theatre, who does not need to create a particular personality. Like the congress convenor, the storyteller has a pedagogic role and the responsibility for ensuring aims are accomplished. The storyteller is a powerful pedagogic tool for communicating the people's knowledge and wisdom (Chinyowa, 2001).

Simon Callow's performance in *The Mystery of Charles Dickens* included at least twenty different roles. He moved between a narrator, Charles Dickens, and a multitude of Dickens' characters as diverse as O'Toole's. Callow as the narrator and O'Toole as the congress convenor concealed the mechanics of performing their roles but, in others, skills were exposed. Their approaches to roles varied.

The moment of the leaves of history was 'a theatrical moment' and yet it was not within the dramatic fiction. O'Toole found most 'emotional commitment' in this moment of the session. While there are some parallels between this and acting (language, voice, gesture) Kirby and Hodge, as we saw in chapter 2, both distinguish acting as requiring an impersonation, and would identify this moment as an example of performing.

Comment

The comparison between teacher roles and theatrical roles can be extended. In theatre different roles require different approaches and, in this case study, the same applied to the drama class. Unlike O'Neill, O'Toole believes that role can be highly theatrical and can elaborate on the text, and unlike O'Neill, he plays a host of different types of role. O'Toole's roles covered a broader range on Kirby's Acting and Non-Acting continuum. He used a few elements of acting for the congress convenor and many for the three named characters. So there is no consensus between O'Neill and O'Toole's practice despite their same drama training background.

However, despite the difference in practice there is a similar discourse. While O'Toole argues for minimalist roles that don't take attention, arguably in all three named roles, O'Toole was the centre of attention, and the roles were far from minimalist. Indeed, the students clapped after O'Toole finished playing Jack McCann. In these cases, the fiction placed him in front of the participants in his own space at a distance from them.

The semiotic analysis and examination of roles and approaches appear to align O'Toole's teacher-in-role work closely to that of actors. The analysis of function reconfirms my scepticism about an 'innocent', value neutral notion of the function of teacher-in-role and weakens an argument that the function of teacher-in-role is what distinguishes it from acting. Finally, the case study has revealed that there is no consensus about how teacher-in-role is played.

11

Case study – FIONA SHAW

Fiona Shaw was born in Cork in 1958, of an affluent family who enjoyed music and literature. The family was uneasy about her desire to go to drama school, despite her obvious skills. She earned a clutch of drama prizes during her teens but went on to study Philosophy at University College Cork. After this she began her acting training at RADA. Details of her life are important because she believes that an actor's life and performance are drawn together since in their acting 'the history of who you are is in your voice' (2000, Interview).

Indeed, Dominic Cavendish noted 'When she talks ... you see the former philosophy student – rational, intellectually inquisitive and as nervily alert off-stage as on' (*Daily Telegraph*, 15 January, 2001). Shaw maintains association with the academy. As well as receiving an honorary doctorate from the National University of Ireland, she is Honorary Professor of Drama Studies at Trinity College Dublin.

Shaw is unashamedly pro high culture and this is evident when she says, *But I have nothing against popular culture* (cited in Oddey, 1999, p158) and then goes on to speak about weighty plays. Cavendish states that 'she has little time for contemporary playwrights' (2001). She eulogises over the language of the classics and deems *The Wasteland* 'the best text I have ever done, I suppose' (2000, Interview). She is concerned about what she sees as a growing fragmentation of language and clearly considers this a downward step.

She argues that by the beginning of the twentieth century, America *... due to its multinational mix ... had a tendency towards the noun. People would stop using the filigree language of the 18th or 19th Century, because people would come from all over the world going: 'coffee', or 'pizza', 'car', 'money'...*(cited in Zucker, 1999 p158).

Shaw is excited by the dynamic between actor and the audience of stage performance, *enjoying the sense of the audience and its effect on that performance. When you ask me why I do all this, all I know is that it's something to do with rendering. The only way you can get to render yourself is to render everything you know, and the only way you can get to that hopefully is on the terrible challenge of courting failure* (cited in Oddey, 1999 p157). Shaw claims to thrive on the feeling of danger and the risk that is endemic in public performance. In the theatre she senses a raw exhilaration of knowing it is happening in the here and now and nothing can be changed once it has.

Originally earning a reputation for comic work, particularly in the classics, Shaw found that her performance in *Electra* in 1982 changed her working life. She won the Olivier Award for best actress and her performance was recently described by Jennifer Wallace in the *Times Higher Educational Supplement* as one in 'which the audience was moved to tears' (THES 2000). This audience response was surpassed this year when members of the audience were apparently fainting and vomiting in response to her portrayal of the title role in Euripedes' *Medea* (Kellaway, *The Observer Review,* 21 January, 2001).

Shaw performed *Hedda Gabler* in Dublin at the Abbey Theatre as well as in London in1993. It was later televised. Her approach to the role helps us to understand her approach to her work as an actor. Shaw unearths complexities and treats them as quite straightforward. Thus she manages to create a believably neurotic Hedda instead of the more usual portrayal as hard and manipulative. She took Hedda's words, 'I am a coward' as the key to her understanding of the character (cited in Zucker, 1999, p.165) and therefore saw a vulnerable Hedda, someone who knows she is continually making mistakes. Her breathy, stammering performance signed the insecurities, hesitation and impulsiveness she found in the character. She sought out the instances of helplessness, of fear and of inadequacy in Hedda. *It's so uninteresting to judge her as a hard-hearted woman who has all the power* (*ibid* p165).

Shaw's Hedda came about through a fusion between the text and her own life. She claimed to have learnt much about her grandparents and to have drawn for her role on some of her mother's gestures. Her own life seems to have evolved by her work almost taking her by surprise. Although she doesn't take to the character approach that is Stanislavski's legacy, she talks of *experiencing the event.*

So you put yourself in the situation, and you'll discover your character. You don't have a character that walks into the situation. You can't know your character, in fact. You're just you (Zucker, 1999, p160).

Shaw sees the process of preparing for a role as strongly instinctive, *So really, the best actors in the world are those who are often rather simple about what they do: they just do it, they don't plan it or organise it or manipulate it, they just **are** it. It's very near what Peter Brook says about language, it's to find out **what it does for you**, and not **what you do to it*** (*ibid* p157).

Since this case study, Fiona Shaw won the *Evening Standard* best actor award for her performance in *Medea*.

CONTEXT OF OBSERVATION

When	20th June, 2000
With whom	A Dublin audience and an Irish company
Duration	1 hours 40 minutes
Where	The Abbey Theatre, Dublin, Republic of Ireland
Participant numbers and age	Full theatre of 628 seats. Range of ages from early twenties up.
Gender/ethnic mix	Mixed gender, mainly white Irish audience
Space	Large theatre with tiered seating. The set spilled out from the raised stage, so that actors could enter from steps at the front of the auditorium

Experience	The audience were likely to be regular attenders since membership of the theatre is significant at The Abbey
Knowledge of leader	Shaw was presented in the publicity posters and programme as Ireland's own star. Probably many in the theatre knew a fair bit about her life and career

Play outline

The play opens with an explanation by the nurse of what has gone before. We learn that Medea, the daughter of a barbarian king, has special powers. She fell inlove with Jason and helped him and his Argonauts to recover the Golden Fleece, and then fled with him to Corinth, leaving her native Colchis. To aid their escape, Medea killed her brother and tricked the daughters of a usurping king into boiling their father alive. The nurse explains that, having done all this for Jason, he has now abandoned her for the young daughter of King Creon. The nurse is afraid of Medea's reaction. Medea is hurt and angry, and full of violent speech.

Medea does not conceal her anger, and fearful of what she may do, Creon tells her that she and her sons must leave Corinth that very day. She begs for one more day. During this day she arranges asylum for her future with King Aegeus in Athens, and begs Jason to ask the princess to keep and care for their sons. She then sends a present of a poisoned dress to the princess, who is killed along with her father.

After much anguished hesitation, Medea kills her own sons to complete her revenge on Jason. She argues over their bodies with Jason before leaving him bereft of wife, regal father-in-law, status and sons, and flees to Athens.

Semiotic analysis of performance

When exploring the semiotic features of the drama teachers, I compared their teacher-in-role with the role they presented as teacher. In the case of Shaw, I can only compare her role as Medea with the person she presented to me when we met. This slightly alters the implication of the table because when in role as teachers speaking to their classes, O'Neill and O'Toole were aware of a large group and their parallel role as the leader of the session. When I spoke to Shaw, she had only me to address and she had no responsibility for the interview. The grid below attempts to highlight the distinctions between the Shaw who presented herself to me in the interview, and the Shaw who presented herself to an audience at the Abbey Theatre. The role of Medea was naturally more varied than that of Shaw on interview, but I identified certain tendencies throughout the performance.

Personas

Transmitters	Shaw in interview	Shaw as Medea
Oral text	Clear; lines overlapped, interrupted with additional ideas adding to meaning	McLeish translation: direct, and clear, retaining the poetic rhythm
Paralinguistic features	Moderate volume, low pitch and very fast. Use of intonation. Irish accent	Huge variety in volume, rhythm and and gasping. Irish accent
Kinesic factors	Minimal gesture. Use of hands and movements of the head	Huge variety of large gestures eg playing – often violently – with toys, running about, waving arms up to the skies, roughing her sons' hair repeatedly, holding a fixed gesture such as sitting head in hands.
Proxemic relations	On a chair opposite me with a table between us. She put her feet up on the chair beside her, filling more space.	On a raised stage with a distance maintained between audience and actor. Spatial relationships with others varied, from close enough to hug, kiss or kill, to isolated moments of

Transmitters	Shaw in interview	Shaw as Medea
		isolation. She used every part of the designated space.
Vestimentary codes	Shorts, tee shirt and trainers	Elegant, heeled black court shoes with a simple v-necked black dress. A cardigan was worn at the beginning but soon removed as the drama developed.
Properties	None	Toys lay about the stage that Shaw used. At one stage she burnt a teddy bear.

The exaggerated gestures and use of space contributed to the depth of the tragedy, to the build up of tension, and to the poetic language of the translation. The early removal of the cardigan symbolised a removal of constraint. At this early stage it communicated what she was both capable of and prepared to fulfil. It had a similar effect to the act of rolling up sleeves in its sense of being prepared, but it carried this more powerful energy of removing what might hold her back. The toys scattered about the performance space reasserted the innocence and vulnerability of the children, while the toy sailing boat that floated constantly in the square pool was a constant reminder of the ship, *Argos*, and all that Medea had done for Jason.

The moment selected for close scrutiny comes towards the end of the speech in which Medea deliberates about whether or not she can go through with her plan for revenge. She eventually succeeds in talking herself into the action.

Theatrical communication in a moment of drama

The table opposite highlights the complexity of the moment. The lines are of death, yet the action is stroking the womb which is the preparation for life. The words are spoken with determination and strength, yet the stroking of the stomach reveals vulnerability. There is murderous intention in front of our eyes, yet we are encouraged to see the blame as lying elsewhere. It is the juxtaposition of the oral text and the action that creates the contradictions that in turn problematise a simple verdict of guilty. I have chosen this moment for analysis, because for me it acts as a microcosm of this Deborah Warner production.

The interview

Shaw spoke at length about the play and its relevance to our society. She explained her defensiveness of Medea, the wronged woman, and drew contemporary parallels and identified implicit contemporary questions raised in this production. But for the purpose of this thesis, I select the parts of the interview in which she expresses her view of acting. In addition to *Medea*, she refers to her solo performance of *The Wasteland*.

Encoding of meaning				Decoding of meaning		
Source of information	Oral text	Paralinguistic register	Kinesic factors	Meaning	Intention	Desired audience reaction
Shaw	'I must kill the children quickly and be gone.'	Steady rhythm, no pauses, smooth enunciation. Deliberately spoken	Stroking lower stomach in a circling motion.	I feel the pain of knowing these children are of his womb. I feel my motherhood.	To demonstrate the killer is not without feeling – is still a mother, not a heartless monster.	To look and be angry at what has pushed a loving mother to this.

To explain her concept of acting, Shaw drew my attention to the two children in the production and told me about how they had been selected. For Shaw, what was sought in children is important in adult actors too.

> Children are a very good template for saying perhaps everything about what acting might be. As soon as a child says 'well I put my hands through my hair and was blind' they have been corrupted somehow, like Adam and Eve! They've lost this thing. Really, acting is the opposite, it's about reacting, it's about being, so it's about listening, it's about responding and therefore fundamentally changing nightly. The worry about any pattern of learned behaviour is it's dead when it's connected to text

She added that the children used in the play 'were not needy'. They did not need to feel the attention of the audience or the other actors, 'they just seem to be rather robust members of humanity, lucky possibly!' I wondered if it had anything to do with skill.

> Oh no no! In fact, it will be healthy to not have skills.

> When it comes to murder, no there is no gesture. I think gesture's the killer actually; a gesture follows a thought – the thought leads. It's their innocence that is the thing that gets caught the minute they start doing innocent acting.

> The boys are emblematic in this play. They aren't real people, but will have to signify something – they have to represent the perfect boys, lovely sons, committed sons.

I asked how this compared to what actors do.

> I think adults are drawing on their experience or their imaginative experience as it's meant to be, if experience, and what is very tricky about adult acting is that the history of your voice is in your voice, the history of who you are is in your voice, people with big lives make potentially very good actors. People who have an imaginative ability to transform ordinary experience into something poetical or theatrical.

Shaw spoke about different types of role, distinguishing between social and professional roles and the role of Medea in the play. She moves from these roles to her role as the actor.

You are playing the role of interviewer now but you also are the interviewer now, I mean, whether you play it or not, you could say 'well for this interview I think I had better wear a three piece suit' – you would be heightened in both sense of role, but as you are just wearing a tee shirt, you think 'well, I just am the interviewer'. I think our theatre is getting much nearer that. In a second if I asked you a lot of questions, there might be a query from the outside as to which one of us was the interviewer. That would be my hijacking the role of interviewer, wouldn't it? There is a role in Medea, but the function of the role... I don't know what it is. I mean it's not to carry any message. It is to release Medea as my role. As an actress my role is to release the role of Medea.

About actor/audience relationships she said:

There are some very unfortunate actors who so ignore audience – they don't perform for them. I've seen some actors here making decisions about 'I don't really want to come out from behind this thing', but if you don't come out from behind this thing, you've lost sight of for whom you are doing it.

She herself feels that at the back of your mind you are absolutely in conversation with the audience. Regarding deceit and the role of the actor, Shaw explained:

Cicely Berry always says the thing about texts, is that it is as easy to lie as to tell the truth, but of course, actually all acting is lying ... I am Medea. There's a truth in that.

I asked Shaw about playing Richard II.

It was very hard. I didn't expect it to be so hard. It wasn't eventually; eventually I did male for a year, you wear down the boundary but initially I was just asking them to do something that I didn't believe. It was only at the beginning, it wasn't really about the entire play. It was just really hard to come on, say those words (because the audience make an instant decision in about ten seconds) in that first ten seconds.

I wondered how Shaw might compare what she did when performing Medea to what she did when presenting/reading *The Wasteland*.

Acting is not about words really, it's about the freedom, it's about action and it's about the three dimensions of those words. But people say the words do it, of course they don't. It's what you feel about the words that does it. It's your imagination and even if you never believe it, if you think imaginatively enough the words will come off that colour – that's the miracle of it. You know, if you think that the orange juice is a bomb; if you call it the orange juice and you're thinking 'bomb', it changes the word. It's all about investment.

About working on *The Wasteland* with Deborah Warner, she said, 'Of course, it was about what ever you want it to be about'. She said she was watching it like a movie in front of her eyes. I wondered if a literary scholar would have read it differently.

I'm not even interpreting it. I am responding to it. and I am not expecting my response to it to be yours. I respond to it, explode it in a way that I hope will explode quite differently in your mind. A literary scholar is telling you – is doing what I am doing, but telling you that is the truth. [I'm making] it occur so it is alive. That's all. I'm making it alive. Once it's alive the meanings jump off. Not to look for meanings is the thing.

Shaw was pleased to play a character again, in *Medea*.

In *Medea* there is a chance to play a person. It is the past. The real play is the story of a fantastic journey, fantastic falling in love and a woman who loves too much, and an absolute self-sacrifice; giving up everything for somebody, which isn't really her fault and something she never takes on in the play. She says 'it's you started it', in fact she should never, ever – and she says that herself, 'I should never have left my home' – but also 'I should have never killed my brother'. I mean, there are certain things that you should not do for another person...These things are where our emotions still do lie and if we can take the consequence and make it clear in a sympathetic way. So it's a different exercise to *The Wasteland.*

Analysis of interview

The interview can be analysed in terms of what Shaw sees as significant in acting, and what she deems inappropriate in acting. Some of the points on the table below she explains explicitly; others are implicit.

Shaw interview: Good Acting

SHAW'S VIEW	EVIDENCE
Acting is being in the moment and responding to what comes	*It's about reacting; it's about being; so it's about listening; it's about responding and therefore fundamentally changing nightly*
Not repeated patterns or learnt behaviour	*The worry about any pattern of learned behaviour is it's dead when it's connected to text*
Instinctive physical responses to intellectual activity	*I think gesture's the killer actually; a gesture follows a thought – the thought leads*
Making use of personal or imagined experiences	*I think adults are drawing on their experience or their imaginative experience*
More enriched by lived experience	*People with big lives are potentially very good actors*
Transforming the ordinary into the poetic or theatrical	*People who have an imaginative ability to transform ordinary experience into something poetical or theatrical*
Releasing the fictional role	*As an actress my role is to release the role of Medea*
A performance for the benefit of the audience	*If you don't come out from behind this thing, you've lost sight of for whom you are doing it*
A relationship with the audience which can enable communication to take place between character and audience, even behind the back of other characters. It is therefore a duality of performance, operating for both the other roles and for the audience	*The signal is one thing to him* [Jason], *but something else to you* [the audience]

SHAW'S VIEW	EVIDENCE
A deceit	*Actually, all acting is lying*
Having to believe what you expect the audience to believe. Approaching the role with conviction	Re. the audience accepting her role as Richard II: *Initially I was asking them to do something that I didn't believe*
More than words. It is the conviction and investment that creates belief beyond words or objects themselves	*Acting is not about words really. It's about freedom; it's about action and it's about the three dimensions of these words ... if you think imaginatively enough the words will come off that colour – that's the miracle of it.* *If you think that the orange juice is a bomb; if you call it the orange juice and you're thinking 'bomb', it changes the word. It's all about investment*

This table makes it clear that acting requires a response to what is taking place and is not regurgitating what has been planned. A fresh performance each night implies close communication with the audience and with other actors. Gestures are not predetermined – they move from thought. Learnt behaviour on stage is deemed the death of the action. In the table above, I described this as being 'in the moment'. This phrase is used frequently by Johnstone, who coined the term 'playing in the moment'. The fact that Johnstone's term was applied to improvisation gives an interesting dimension on Shaw's view of acting. She expresses in the interview a notion of acting as fresh and re-created, rather than learnt and delivered.

The interview also reveals the close relationship between mental investment and what is communicated to an audience. The implication is that if the actor believes in what she is doing, the audience will also believe it. The mental commitment is more important than specific acting skills. Shaw does not refer to acting skills, and dismissed them categorically in relation to child performers. What is crucial, which is perhaps more than a learnt skill, is the ability to transform the everyday into something 'artistic'.

Shaw did not explain what she meant by this, but I propose she was referring to something we considered in Section One, the conscious way of making an action significant that makes it a theatrical rather than a social act.

'Acting has its own coherent body of statements that similarly produce a self-confirming account of the reality of the acting process'. The discourse Shaw has drawn upon clearly makes assumptions about me (her audience) and involves concepts set up with which to analyse acting. This discourse appears to be a particular discourse that is prevalent among contemporary actors, and provides a stark contrast to Mamet's which is far more down to earth. Shaw's observation: 'Being a performer is not a job, it's a philosophy, and it is an alternative life in a way to the structured life of ordinary people' (cited in Oddey, 1999, p153) highlight the discourse and its distinction from Mamet's examined earlier.

Shaw explains that her function as an actress is to *release the role of Medea*. This phrase warrants examination. The idea of a character being released seems to suppose that there is an existing character waiting to be released. This cuts against the common view of a character being constructed through the interaction between text, actor, production and audience interpretation (Aston and Savona, 1991). It also conflicts with the production itself. This production derived from a particular feminist position. Shaw spoke of her defensiveness of Medea. It presented a different Medea from Eileen Hurley's 'archetypal woman scorned' at the Globe in 1948, and from Diana Rigg's award winning performance of 1996. These women have released 'Medeas' rather than 'Medea'. Indeed, in the interview Shaw explained that her interpretation in acting roles will not be the same as others' interpretations.

> I think adults are drawing on their experience or their imaginative experience and what is very tricky about adult acting is that the history of who you are is in your voice. People with big lives make potentially very good actors.

As one outside the actor's discourse, I find myself challenging some of the notions of acting that Shaw offers. I am not convinced that *the history of who you are is in your voice*, nor how this is squared with a view that *people with big lives make potentially very good actors*, since those big lives will be carried in their voices and may therefore restrict their range. This somewhat complex claim about adult actors goes against her notion of children as a template for acting. Shaw described the strength of an innocent acting style that allows thought to lead gesture and enables the freedom to respond and react. Big lives making good actors seems to be a contradiction to the uncorrupted, pre Adam and Eve idea of good acting. Shaw herself alludes to the fact that what she describes appears to be without solid rationality: 'If you think imaginatively enough the words will come off that colour – that's the miracle of it.'

Contextualising the case study

Early in this book I proposed that there is a particular view of theatre that has led to a particular perception of acting. I argued that this view of acting has contributed to the assertion that teacher-in-role is not acting and suggested alternative forms that are more akin to teacher-in-role. However, this case study provides an example of that particular western view of theatre. It fulfils the criteria for the traditional model, without audience participation, without improvisation, and with no application to a specific context with intended outcomes. In research terms, then, I set out to give myself the biggest challenge by using a case study which seemed as far away as it could be, conceptually at least, from drama in education.

Contexts and audience relationships – Walking into a theatre venue like the Abbey, expectations are of a silent audience, and a performance that operates in a space removed from the audience in some way, usually a raised stage. These expectations were fulfilled in Warner's production. The audience expected to be entertained even though most would have been aware that it might be 'heavy'. Although the production offered some unexpected humour, these expectations were also fulfilled. While some audience members might have been interested to learn about a Greek myth, the majority probably expected to have not a learning experience but a thought-provoking and emotional one.

Shaw saw the play as very important to its audience:

We need tragedy at the moment. We're living in very confusing times. We're losing by the moment the power of debate. 'Medea' is pertinent to all of us at the moment. People do kill their children. This play asks, 'How can this happen?' As a society, we like to believe that children come first. They absolutely don't. Adult relationships come first. Passion comes first. (cited in Cavendish, 2001)

Perhaps her expectations for the play were slightly different from the audience's. There is a hint of the preacher or teacher in her words.

But in terms of contexts and audience relationships, this dramatic encounter is very different from the previous two and indicates that Shaw and the teachers are doing very different things. The differences include: a silent audience; separate audience and performance space; very large audiences; no personal familiarity with the actor; no familiarity with most of those in the auditorium; an audience of mixed age groups; an audience who had different reasons for being in the theatre seats (whereas the previous groups shared motives). The only aspect of similarity is the desire of the actor, like the teachers', to communicate about an issue that she believes is important.

Functions and aims – It is clear that Shaw took on the role with commitment to the challenge she expected it to give her. Although she believed that this production had particular aims, *her* aim was obviously to succeed in that challenge. Warner and Shaw's aim for the production appears to have been to begin a debate about how it is possible for parents to kill their children. Consequently Medea is portrayed as a sympathetic character. Let us examine the functions involved.

Functions of the drama

The function of the actor is inevitably caught up with the aim. To bring about a debate about child killers, the actor had to depict Medea as a mother *driven* to kill her sons, so that rather than a child killer she is seen as a woman driven by cruelty; a victim of Jason. The table on page 152 shows Shaw's view of the actor's function. Otherwise this might be seen as finding the complexities of a

The function of the actor	'to liberate the role'
The function of the actor in role	to evoke sympathy for Medea, the child killer
The function of the role	To bring about the tragedy. For Propp, Medea would be 'the dispatcher'.

character and the way to create an appropriate portrayal in the context of the given production. Shaw's suggestion that her function is to 'liberate the role' assumes that there is a particular role to be liberated. Thus we see the same sort of assumption masquerading as consensus that we noted in the earlier case studies. Again, it is difficult to distinguish between the character and the function of the character. Medea's actions determine what we perceive of her character and, at the same time, her actions are what generate the unfolding tragic inevitability.

Skills

With regard to the skills identified in the literature of drama in education, Shaw shows differently from the two teachers. The points in bold in the chart opposite are skills Shaw actually exhibited, and those in italics represent skills which could be conceptualised in her work. If 'participants' is interpreted as the co-actors, as children might be in a classroom drama, then Shaw, too, employed those skills. Two skills I could not identify are those concerned with the creation of the piece and the text in advance of the dramatic event. Warner implies that Shaw was part of the development of the piece: 'She pushes me to places I wouldn't otherwise go. She inspires trust and there has to be trust there for you to free-fall without a parachute. She also has an enormous appetite balanced by being a visceral performer' (cited in Smurthwaite, 2000). This suggests that Shaw played a part in the development of the performance but did not have overall responsibility in the way both the education practitioners did.

SKILLS EXHIBITED BY SHAW

Skills employed from the sphere of drama in education	structuring the drama like a dramatist **signing through voice** **communicating through gesture** improvisation skills: spontaneity, narration skills, selection of significant parts of the oral text as a playwright **listening to the participants** **responding to the participants**
Skills employed from the sphere of acting	
	a) develop and play a character in rehearsals and performances and sustain it before an audience within the framework of a production as directed
	b) show evidence of skills of characterisation
	c) create believable character and emotion appropriate to the demands of the text and production
	d) define the objectives of a character and embody and express these within the context of a production
	e) make full use of individuality in performance
	f) work sensitively with other actors in rehearsal and performance
	g) show evidence in performance of creative imagination, emotion, thought, concentration and energy
	h) develop an effective working process and the ability to monitor and evaluate its application
	i) make use of personal experience and observation to assist in the creation of role

j) prepare and sustain the quality of concentration necessary for each performance

l) use make-up, costumes and props effectively to develop performance

m) communicate to an audience with expression, emotion and spontaneity

n) adjust to the demands of different venues and media

p) read and interpret text with accuracy and confidence

s) study text, in both prose and verse, and make full use of the structures and phrasing in order to reveal character, intention and the development of a story

t) create and sustain an improvised rehearsal or performance with discipline and spontaneity

The number of skills exhibited from the acting list is extensive, as is true of O'Toole and, to a slightly lesser extent, O'Neill.

All three also operated the rhythm and pace of the drama in which they took part. Because so many of the skills listed are relevant to all three case study subjects, the distinction between the two activities again, blurs.

Approaches – It is clear from what Shaw said, as well as from her performance, that she had made mental preparation for the role of Medea. That internal process that Morgan and Saxton speak about seemed more significant than external considerations. No special walks or voices were adopted: Shaw's gestures and expression communicated the internal turmoil. As Shaw explained, her approach to the role was to ensure thought led to gesture, rather than the other way round, so the external features appeared a result of the internal state.

As we saw, States identifies one mode of performance as 'self-expressive'. Roles that invited this type of performance included

Medea and, in some senses, Shaw's artistry did indeed become the focus of audience attention. His observation that 'we react to the actor's particular way of doing this role' (1996, p22) fits my experience in the audience. But also relevant to Shaw's performance are States' descriptions of his 'representational mode'. As mesmerising as Shaw's performance was, so too was the content of the play. It 'is now an enactment of significant human experience ... the virtuosity now lies in the power of the subject, the collaboration in the mutual agreement by actor and audience on the value and appropriateness of the subject to the community of men' (*ibid*, p35). As well as admiring Shaw's skill in the role, I also moved in and out of seeing her merge into Medea, the role. There seemed to be some conflict at play. On the one hand, the play itself promotes a self-expressive mode, in line with Aston and Savona's notion of the personated character prevalent in the classic texts of ancient Greece. On the other hand, Shaw's performance did not invite a distinction between actor and role. Again, distinctions prove difficult. Shaw's performance does not neatly match the theoretical classifications.

Comment

This case study of an actor brought interesting surprises. Firstly, it revealed certain similarities in the performance of practitioners of drama in education and actors. Secondly, there seems to be a degree of overlap regarding Shaw's notion of functions and aims. Thirdly, the theoretical distinctions between types of approach to performance have emerged as fragile. Classifying Shaw's performance has not been straightforward. This fits with the view considered in Section One that most performances are hybrids, drawing upon different approaches and blending them as required in the specific piece.

The book concludes with comparisons between the case studies and their implications are analysed.

CONCLUSION
ANALYSES AND POSSIBILITIES

Certain conclusions can be drawn from the case studies. They are followed by more general consideration of the researched theory and practice and the implications for my argument.

Views of acting

O'Neill made distinctions between teacher-in-role and acting. Below are the main points as compared with Shaw's view of acting. When set alongside Shaw's notion of acting, O'Neill's distinctions do not appear to hold. Given that Shaw's *Medea* represents a conventional theatre form and acting style, her view should comply with O'Neill's description of acting, but it does not. In fact, what emerges is that there are profound similarities between O'Neill's view of teacher-in-role and Shaw's view of acting.

Relating two views: O'Neill and Shaw

O'NEILL'S VIEW OF TIR AND ACTING	SHAW'S VIEW OF ACTING
TIR responds to what is given, improvises so is not fixed by a script, as an actor is	Acting is about responding and listening and therefore the performance will change nightly
TIR avoids seeking attention, but acting demands to be the focus of attention	Specifically argues for children who are not needy of attention (children are a template for acting). They should not demand attention

O'NEILL'S VIEW OF TIR AND ACTING	SHAW'S VIEW OF ACTING
TIR maintains a distance from the role. An actor embodies the role.	Shaw is critical of actors who forget that their priority is to perform for an audience, so the role does not take over this primary aim. She implies some distance. Shaw also speaks of signing to the audience and to other characters, which suggests a remove from embodying the character.
TIR works through representation while an actor becomes the character	*The boys are emblematic in this play. They aren't real people, but will have to signify something – they have to represent the perfect boys, lovely sons, committed sons*
Unlike acting, TIR is functional	The function of the actor is *to liberate the role.* The role is played in a production that has a particular feminist position, which implies a particular function for the role of Medea. She functions to bring sympathy for her position and anger against Jason's. She functions as the protagonist, who fulfils the tragedy
TIR is simple, but acting is elaborate and complex	Acting requires an innocence likened to before the corruption of Adam and Eve. Shaw admires simple portrayal – *I think gesture is the killer, actually*

Thus there are clearly similarities between O'Neill's view of teacher-in-role and Shaw's view of acting. It is also the case that in some respects O'Neill's conception of teacher-in-role differs from what Shaw does. So how does O'Toole's view of teacher-in-role relate to Shaw's view of acting?

In the table below, the left hand column shows O'Toole's list of possibilities for teacher-in-role. In the next two columns I identify the degree to which O'Neill and Shaw comply with O'Toole's possibilities. 'Agree' denotes that the point was articulated or revealed in practice. 'Disagree' means that the point was opposed in the interview or not carried out in practice. Interestingly, there is a little discrepancy in the degree to which Shaw admires minimalism in the interview yet does not play a minimalist role as Medea.

Relating three views: O'Toole, O'Neill and Shaw

O'Toole on teacher-in-role	O'Neill on teacher-in-role	Shaw on acting
Can use costume	disagree	agree
Can use properties	disagree	agree
Can use space theatrically	disagree	agree
Can involve emotional commitment	disagree	agree
Can be a character	disagree	agree
Should not draw attention	agree	agree
Played in a minimalist way	agree	agree in interview but performance was not minimalist

The table is interesting because it suggests that paradoxically O'Toole's notion of teacher-in-role is closer to Shaw's notion of acting than to O'Neill's view of teacher-in-role. This table supports the argument that the practices of teacher-in-role are plural rather than monolithic. Were we to analyse particular roles, we would find different results. O'Toole's congress convenor was very like O'Neill's congress convenor, but he played a range of roles that were quite different.

So O'Neill's view of acting is not shared by Shaw. However, her view of teacher-in-role has some similarities with Shaw's notion of acting. O'Toole's view of teacher-in-role goes a long step closer to

Shaw's view of acting. While one of his roles is very close to O'Neill's, his other roles are theoretically closer to Shaw's view of acting.

Role of actor and teacher in the drama event

It may be argued that the distinctions between the kind of input made by actor and teacher are so different that the comparisons have serious limitations. Earlier I considered the additional roles often ascribed to the teacher in the overall drama event, such as director and playwright, and pointed out that although these theatrical roles were identified as part of teacher-in-role, acting was not mentioned.

There are issues concerning the director and the playwright. Did Shaw have any influence on the overall production in a directorial sense? The director of *Medea*, Deborah Warner, is a friend of Fiona Shaw and they have worked together many times. 'They say they only do plays they don't know how to do' (Smurthwaite, 2001 p20). This implies joint endeavour and shared responsibility for the piece. That does not mean Warner is opting out of her directorial responsibilities, rather that she favours a contemporary approach of an ensemble production. Hitchcock, like Mamet, would not have expected his leading actor to interfere with what he saw as his responsibility, but Warner clearly expects contributions and experimentation with the actors. 'Warner ... says Shaw is much cleverer than she is 'which makes her a great person to have in the rehearsal room" (*ibid*). I suggest that since the actor may have an eye to the direction of a piece of drama, she may, like the teacher, be thinking of more than just her own role presentation. We saw that Shaw's performance exemplifies this in a traditional production. Clearly, other theatre pieces will have been constructed even more collaboratively.

The second issue concerns the scripted nature of Shaw's performance. She worked from the translation of Euripides' text by McLeish. O'Neill said she worked from a script at the beginning of her drama – she knew what she was going to say. She thought that she later responded to what the participants offered and changed the way she replied to them accordingly. O'Toole also responds to what he is given by participants. In this sense, both 'devised' their own 'dramas' and both had taught them many times before my observation, so they knew their scripts and they knew what they might expect from the participants. I wonder how much the way they respond in role varies. I have asked two drama practitioners who experienced the same dramas about what took place. Apparently the differences in what took place were slight. I know that in my own practice I have taught the same drama and only rarely encountered radically different developments. More usually, they were only minor.

Arguably, teachers-in-role are also writing as they go, because they have to respond to the moment. Shaw, like the teachers-in-role, works from a text. The script was not her own but once she is acting and the teachers are in role, does it matter who wrote the script? Much teacher-in-role work by teachers uses someone else's 'script'. O'Neill and O'Toole have both published drama lessons which provide scripts for teachers to use. This surely doesn't change our concept of their teacher roles. Some of the classroom dialogue may well be written through improvisation as the teacher responds to the participants. Shaw expresses concern about response – just as the teachers do: 'Acting is about reacting, it's about being, so it's about listening, it's about responding and therefore fundamentally changing nightly.' Shaw, too, anticipates being flexible and like teachers believes that the performances change each time.

However much the degree to which the 'texts' were pre-planned fluctuates, a key commonality is that each of the case study subjects has created performance texts. Furthermore, each describes a processual concept of that performance text and expects to respond in the moment. And each expects to change and develop their roles during each 'performance'. This takes us to the heart of another opposition in drama in education. The process and product dichotomy emerges as insignificant in the light of Shaw's explanation of her work. For the actor, as for the teachers, there is no sense of a final, completed dramatic encounter. Reforming and reshaping is part of the event for future occasions. There is no finality in their concepts of the event that makes it only a 'product'. If each 'performance' is part of the on-going process, these oppositional boundaries blur.

Though other theatrical forms may be closer to the teacher-in-role led drama of the classroom, it is impossible to ignore similarities. Actor and teachers in these case studies have both been concerned with the overall drama, both have spoken at least to some degree to a pre-planned script, and both see themselves responding in the moment and adjusting their roles accordingly.

These case studies provide a unique opportunity to compare teacher-in-role with the work of an actor. The data on the skills involved in the activities is particularly interesting. The list of acting criteria provided a system for identifying the skills of teacher-in-role and revealed that our actor and teachers were using common skills to perform their roles. While the acting skills were not applicable solely to the actor, similarly the teachers in-role held no monopoly over the skills identified in this book as associated with teacher-in-role. Little has been written about the skills required to use teacher-in-role, and this is perhaps another reason – one I had not predicted – that teacher-in-role was seen as distinctly different from acting. In the light of the common skills identified here, however, it is time to reconsider.

Overview

There has been reluctance in drama in education to see teacher-in-role as acting behaviour. Although Bolton, in *Acting in Classroom Drama,* has endorsed a view of the roles participants play as acting behaviour, the teacher's roles have consistently been distanced from it. Indeed, when I first discussed my research idea with colleagues in the field most of them suggested that it would be better to look at the functions of teacher-in-role. This book questions such orthodoxy.

I began by examining the literature in drama in education, where I identified a position which revealed the orthodoxy. I then began to question the sharp contrasts it makes between teacher-in-role and acting. When the literature of the two fields are juxtaposed we see that the images of theatre within drama in education are limited. Many forms of theatre are neglected, particularly those close to drama in education, such as the various participatory forms, and applied theatre contexts which have a particular purpose, raising issues or imparting information. The narrow concept of theatre results in an equally limited concept of acting which excludes even the improvisation actor, despite the marked overlap with the teacher-in-role. In contrast, I found contemporary theory on acting inclusive and open, offering definitions and categories on the understanding that they are temporary.

This contrast seems odd, particularly when drama in education is a discipline that has recently sought to justify its practice by aligning itself explicitly with theatre forms. The vocabulary of the field has increasingly incorporated more theatrical terminology, while practice is conceptualised through theatrical models. However, despite teacher-in-role being for a long time identified with the roles of playwright and director, the recent reconsiderations have not provoked a reconceptualisation of teacher-in-role as akin to acting. How strange that the most likely connection has been omitted! So I wish to introduce to the growing re-evaluations within the field a concept of teacher-in-role as a form of acting.

Examining the literature of both fields first revealed the difference in approach to definitions. Whereas theatrical theory resists strict definitions so as to incorporate broad ranging and developing practices, drama in education appears to assume a consensus around a specific practice which entails closed and fixed definitions. In order to systemise the theoretical analysis, I selected four areas in the literature of drama in education that appear to be key to the distinctions between teacher-in-role and acting. Within all four areas – context and audience relationships, functions and aims, skills, and approaches – concepts were derived from a narrow perception of theatre and acting theory presented notions of practice that rendered such definitions and distinctions unsustainable.

Having constructed a theoretical argument for blurring the distinction between teacher-in-role and acting, I applied it to practice by means of the case studies. The systematic application of theoretical frameworks facilitated this process, exposed some discrepancy between discourse and practice and indicated that no sharp distinction could be made between teacher-in-role and acting.

To enable the theoretical analysis of practice, I constructed systems that would bring teacher-in-role into a theatrical frame of reference so both would be examined through the same analytical lens. This was achieved partly by considering practice in the light of the theories set out in Section One and, more specifically, through semiotic analysis. Again it was evident that a tight boundary cannot be drawn between teacher-in-role and acting.

Implications of the research

The list below includes some points that could be anticipated and others that were a surprise.

This research reveals that

- the literature of drama in education has not identified teacher-in-role with acting

- the literature of the field has consistently distanced teacher-in-role from acting

- most of the literature of the field reiterates a narrow concept of acting relevant only to a particular form of traditional western theatre

- there are many other theatre forms which exhibit much in common with drama in education

- in the literature teacher-in-role is deemed different from acting because it has a different function

- roles in classroom dramas and in theatrical performances function similarly

- many skills evident in actor Shaw's performance are also evident in the roles played by teachers O'Neill and O'Toole

- actor and teachers-in-role communicated in similar ways

- there is no consensus about how teacher-in-role is played. O'Neill expresses a concern for only one type of role and one approach to playing it, whereas O'Toole uses a range of role types and approaches

- the aims and functions for teacher-in-role remain similar and intertwined, whatever the approach to the roles.

This research suggests that a reconsideration of teacher-in-role has several implications.

- The field of drama in education should broaden its concepts of both acting and theatre so that acting for the teacher-in-role can cease to be taboo, just as 'theatre' in classroom drama once was.

- The function of teacher-in-role is not as innocent as it purports to be and warrants extended research. Aims and functions appear to be tightly entwined. Such research could seek to determine what kinds of values underpin practice. It would be interesting to see if practitioners tend to operate within tight ideological parameters, as has been suggested, for example, by Nicholson (1995).

- The systemised semiotic analysis constructed here has potential to support further research. Further exploration using this method could produce a closer understanding of the semiotic communication at play between teacher-in-role and participants. Signs are not always decoded as intended. A semiotic analysis could lead to deeper understanding of the unintended signs that have altered the intended meaning. It would give teachers who use role a closer understanding of their own practice. The system could provide a useful enrichment to the reflective practitioner approach espoused by Taylor (1996, 2000).

- Teacher-in-role in classroom drama can be more fully understood and deconstructed through the application of theory from the field of performance.

- There are discrepancies between discourse as espoused by drama practitioners and their practice in the classroom.

The relevance for those of us in drama in education

There are five areas in which this research might be significant.

Liberating practice – This research has compared the conceptualisations of acting found within theatrical discourses to those within the literature of drama in education. What has emerged as striking is the determination of theorists to avoid making strict definitions and distinctions. Zarrilli's view of the temporary definition enables a fluidity in theorising practice. It enables practice to reshape, develop and experiment because it does not expect theatre practice to remain static. If change and rebirth are anticipated, then definitions must shift and reshape to accommodate the evolution. But in the field of drama in education, definitions of teacher-in-role tend to reflect a static concept of practice. What is defined and classified is not expected to expand, experiment and grow in unexpected directions. Such concepts make the practice of drama in education appear strait-jacketed. Thus the research suggests the need for a conceptual freeing up which may lead to a liberation in practice. Practice in the field need not remain static, creating imitations of what has gone before: as with theatre, it can develop, experiment and grow as the living art it is.

Acting is allowed – The second area of significance is allied to the first. Students are influenced by theory. If they are told that teacher-in-role is not acting, their practice may be influenced by that belief. Teachers have possibly been limiting themselves by this assumption. Perhaps this research might re-orientate this pattern and legitimise innovative practice which otherwise might not have been attempted. I do not suggest that students should have actor training. Neither do I suggest that external acting skills should be used excessively, nor that teachers should necessarily use as many costumes as O'Toole. Rather I suggest that teachers should understand that they can draw upon the work of actors to find what is appropriate in their drama and in their context. This is what Heathcote seems to have implied when she wrote 'Signs (and portents?)' back in 1982, but somehow it became lost among the other important aspects of the article.

Acknowledging ideologies – This research has deconstructed the myth of value neutrality and raised questions about purpose. It is significant for foregrounding our need to be able to defend our value choices and reflect upon the possibility that we are more imprisoned in our value system than we think. This research supports Winston's call for reflexivity, a reflexive awareness of where we position ourselves ideologically and how this impinges on our practice (1998, p.84). 'There is no such thing as neutral or unbiased. The challenge is to become as aware as possible of one's own stances in relation to the positions of others and take steps to maintain or change positions' (Schechner, 2002, p2).

A further significance of this research project is its contribution to the new paradigm which seeks to align drama in education with theatre. It has invited a new perspective on the practices of teacher-in-role, giving them the attention that has previously been given to the participants in drama but not to the teacher-in-role.

The missing link – Finally, there might be a conceptual significance even when no change in practice is necessary or desired. Theorising the teacher-in-role as acting may enable teachers to acknowledge the value of different aspects of their experience. After I first read a paper about this work at the Ohio International Drama in Education Research Institute in 2000, Mary Pratt Cooney sent me an email articulating the personal, individual significance of the project that I myself had not understood at the time:

> I remember the moments following your presentation, when people around me, in almost hushed whispers, confessed that they had been actors at one point in their careers. There was something quite liberating about the whole thing. Maybe this provided the 'missing link': permission to connect what had first brought us into the world of theatre with process drama work ... So for the past few years I have felt I was straddling two worlds. Theatre: the production and Theatre: the process. Your paper provided reassurance that they might be reconciled after all. *(Pratt Cooney, email 2000)*

References

Abercrombie, D. (1968) 'Paralanguage', *British Journal of Disorders of Communication*, 3, pp55-59.

Ackroyd, J. (1994) 'A Crack in the Ice: Planning for Secure Drama' *Language and Learning*, Nov/Dec edition.

Ackroyd, J. (1998a) 'The Plant, the Jacket and the Rosary Beads: Objects as Distancing Devices' in O'Sullivan, C. and Williams, G. (eds) *Bridges. Laying the Foundations for a Child Centred Curriculum in Drama and Education*, Birmingham, NATD.

Ackroyd, J. (1998b) 'Much Ado About Shakespeare' in C. Miller and J. Saxton (eds) *The NADIE Journal: Selected IDIERI papers*, Volume 22, Number 1.

Ackroyd, J. and Boulton, J. (2001) *Drama Lessons for Five to Eleven-Year-Olds*, London, David Fulton.

Alcock, B. (1999) 'We Needn't Bring Any Books Tomorrow' in Clark and Tony Goode (eds) *Assessing Drama*, A Gulbenkian Foundation/National Drama Publication.

Allen, J. (1979) *Drama in Schools*, London, Heinemann.

Archer, W. (1912) *Playmaking: A Manual of Craftsmanship*, London, Chapman and Hall.

Aristotle (1981) *Aristotle's Poetics: A Ttranslation and Commentary for Students of Literature*, Tallahassee, University Presses of Florida.

Aston, E. and Savona, G. (1991) *Theatre as a Sign System*, London, Routledge.

Ball, S (1990) *Politics and Policy Making in Education*, London, Routledge.

Ball, S. (2001) 'The Heart of the Matter: placing the arts at the centre of health promotion' in *Research in Drama Education*, Volume 6, Number 2.

Banham, M (1995) *The Cambridge Guide to Theatre*, Cambridge, Cambridge University Press.

Beckerman, B. (eds) Beckerman, G.B. and Coco, C. (1990) *Theatrical Presentation: Performer, Audience and Act*, New York, Routledge.

Bennett, S. (1997) *Theatre Audiences*, second edition, London, Routledge.

Bentley, E. (1992) *The Theory of the Modern Stage*, London, Penguin.

Berger, A.A. (1991)[1933] *Media Analysis Techniques*, revised edition, London, Sage.

Berry, C. (1987) *The Actor and his Text*, London, Harrap.

Best, D. (2001) 'True fiction' in *Drama*,Winter 2001 Volume 9, Number 1.

Biodun, J. (1984) *The Yoruba Popular Travelling Theatre of Nigeria*, Nigeria Magazine.

Blau, H. (1992) *To All Appearances: Ideology and Performance*, New York, Routledge.

Boal, A. (1979) *Theatre of the Oppressed*, trans. Charles A. and Maria-Odilia Leal McBride, London, Pluto.

Boal, A. (1992) *Games for Actors and Non-Actors*, London, Routledge.

Boal, A. (1995) *The Rainbow of Desire*, trans. Adrian Jackson, London, Routledge.

Bolton, G. (1979) *Towards a Theory of Drama in Education*, London, Longman.

Bolton, G. (1998) *Acting in Classroom Drama: A Critical Analysis*, Stoke on Trent,Trentham Books.

Bolton, G. and Heathcote, D. (1999) *So You Want to use Role-play?* Stoke on Trent,Trentham Books.

Boso, C. (1980) 'Contre 'La mort sucree'', in *Bouffonnaires*, Number 3, May.

Bowell, P. and Heap, B. (2001) *Planning Process Drama*, London, David Fulton.

Brecht, B. (1977) *The Measures Taken and other Lehrstuke*, London, Methuen.

Brecht, B. (1981) [1941] *The Resistable Rise of Arturo Ui*, trans. Ralph Manheim, John Willet and Ralph Manheim (eds). London, Methuen.

Brecht, B (1986) [1950] 'The Street Scene' in *Brecht on Theatre* trans. John Willet, London, Methuen.

Brecht, B. (1986) [1957] 'Theatre for pleasure or theatre for instruction' in *Brecht on Theatre*, trans. John Willet, London, Methuen.

Brook, P. (1990) *The Empty Space*, London, Penguin.

Burke, M. (1995) 'Training the Drama Teacher' in *Canadian Tertiary Drama Education Perspectives on Practice,* Juliana Saxton and Carole Miller (eds), Victoria, University of Victoria.

Callow, S. (1985) *Being An Actor*, Harmondsworth, Penguin.

Carey, J. (1990) 'Teaching in Role and Classroom Power' in *Drama Broadsheet*, Summer, Volume 7, Number 2.

Carlson, M (1996) *Performance: A Critical Introduction*, London, Routledge.

Catoron, Louis E. (1993) *The Elements of Playwriting*, London, Macmillan.

Cavendish, D. (2001 'We need tragedy at the moment' *Daily Telegraph*, 15th January.

Chaikein, J. (1991) *The Presence of the Actor*, New York, Theatre Comm. Group.

Chinyowa, K. (2001) 'The *Sarangano* and Shona Storytelling: and African Theatrical Paradigm' *Studies in Theatre and Performance*,Volume 21, Number 1.

Clifford, J. (1986) *Writing Culture*, Berkeley, University of California Press.

Clipson-Boyles, S. (1998) *Drama in Primary English Teaching*, London, David Fulton.

Cohen, L and Manion, L. (1994) *Research Methods in Education*, fourth edition, London, Routledge.

Copeau, J. (1990) [1916] *Copeau: texts on theatre*, trans.John Rudlin (ed), London, Routledge.

Counsell, C. (1996) *Signs of Performance*, London, Routledge.

Croall, J. (1999) 'Fiona and Bernard go touring' in *Stagewrite*, Royal National Theatre.

Culler, J. (1976) *Saussure*, Glasgow, Fontana.

Davis, D. (1998) Forward to Gavin Bolton *Acting in Classroom Drama*, Stoke on Trent,Trentham Books

Durkheim, E. (1964) [1895] *The Rules of Sociological Method*, New York, The Free Press.

Easthope, A. and McGowan, K. (1992) *A Critical and Cultural Theory Reader*, Buckingham, Open University Press.

Edmiston, B and Wilhelm, B. (2000) *Imagining to Learn: Inquiry, Ethics and Integration Through Drama*, New York, Heinemann.

Elam, K. (1991) *The Semiotics of Theatre and Drama*, London, Routledge.

Emilhovich, C. (1995) Distancing Passion: Narratives in Social Science' in J. Hatch and R.Wisnieski (eds) *Life History and Narrative*, New York, Falmer.

Esslin, M. (1974) *The Theatre of the Absurd*, Harmondsworth, Penguin Books.

Esslin, M. (1978) *The Anatomy of Drama*, London, Abacus.

Esslin, M (1987) *The Field of Drama*, London, Methuen.

Euripides, (1993) *Medea*, New York, Dover Publications.

Euripides, (1981) *The Baccae, in Ten Plays by Euripides*, trans. Moses Hadas and John McLean, London, Bantam.

Eyre, R. (1992) 'Theatre de Complicite', September 1st, The Late Show, BBC.

Eyre, R (1999) cited in Zucker, C. (ed) *In the Company of Actors: Reflections on the Craft of Acting*, London, A & C Black.

Fleming, M. (1997) *The Art of Drama Teaching*, London, David Fulton.

Fortier, M. (1997) *Theory/Theatre an introduction*, London, Routledge.

Foucault, M. (1989) *The Archaeology of Knowledge*, London, Routledge.

Frost, A. and Yarrow, R. (1990) *Improvisation in Drama*, London, Macmillan.

Gallagher, K. (2000) *Drama Education in the lives of Girls: Imagining Possibilities*, Toronto, University of Toronto Press.

Gillham, G. (1974) 'Condercum School Report' for Newcastle upon Tyne LEA (unpublished).

Goffman, E. (1959) *The Presentation of Self in Everyday Life*, London, Penguin.

Goodwin, J. (ed) (1983) *Peter Hall's Diaries*, London, Hamish Hamilton.

Goorney, H. (1981) *The Theatre Workshop Story*, London, Eyre Methuen.

Grotowski, J. (1968) *Towards a Poor Theatre*, London, Methuen.

Haigh, G. (1995) 'Cameo Performances' *Times Educational Supplement*. March 10.

Hall, S. (1992) 'The Question of Cultural Identity' in S. Hall, D. Held, T. McGrew, (eds) *Modernity and its Futures*, Cambridge, Polity Press.

Halliwell, S. (1987) *The Poetics of Aristotle*, Chapel Hill, University of North Carolina Press.

Hare, D. (1976) [1947] *Fanshen*, London, Faber.

Harrop, J. (1992) *Acting*, London, Routledge.

HartNumberll, P. (1987) *The Theatre*, London, Thames and Hudson.

Harwood, R. (1984) *All the World's a Stage*, London, Secker and Warburg.

Hawkes, T. (1977) *Structuralism and Semiotics*, London, Methuen.

Hayman, R. (1977) *How To Read a Play*, London, Metheun.

Heathcote, D. (1967) *Drama in Education*, Newcastle, University of Newcastle.

Heathcote, D. (1970) *Three Looms Waiting*, Omnibus, BBC.

Heathcote, D. (1982) 'Sign (and portents?)' in *SCYPT Journal*, Number 9.

Heck, S.F. and Williams, C.R. (1984) *The Complex Roles of the Teacher: An Ecological Perspective*, New York, Teachers' College Press.

Hilton, J. (1987) *Performance*, London, Macmillan.

Hirsch, F. (1984) *A Method in their Madness: the History of the New York Actor's Studio*, London, W.W.Norton.

Hodge, A. (2000) *Twentieth Century Actor Training*, London, Routledge, Methuen.

Hodgson, J. and Richards, E. (1977) *Improvisation*, London, Methuen.

Hornbrook, D. (1998) *Education and Dramatic Art 2nd Edition*, London, Routledge.

Howe, E. (1992) *The First English Actresses: women and drama 1660-1700*, Cambridge, Cambridge University Press.

Ibsen, H. (1998) *Rosmersholm*, Oxford, Oxford Paperbacks.

Ibsen, H. (1993) *A Doll's House*, in *Plays: Two*, trans. Michael Meyer, London, Methuen.

Inglis, F. (1993) 'The Theatre State and the Idiom of Drama', *Drama and the Making of Meaning*, London, National Drama Publications.

Izzo, G. (1998) Acting Interactive Theatre, Portsmouth, New Hampshire, Heinemann.

Jackson, T. (1993) *Learning Through Theatre: New Perspectives on Theatre in Education*, second edition, London, Routledge.

Johnstone, K. (1981) *Impro: Improvisation and the Theatre,* London, Methuen.

Johnstone, K. (1999) *Impro for Storytellers*, London, Faber and Faber.

Kellaway, K. (2001) 'The mother of all tragedies' *The Observer Review,* 21 January.

Kempe, A. (1990) *The GCSE DRAMA Coursebook*, Oxford, Blackwell.

Kerr, D. (1995) 'Theatre for Development' in *African Popular Theatre*, London, Heinemann.

Kirby,M. (1987) A Formalist Theatre, Philadelphia, University of Pennsylvania Press.

Kirby, M. (1996) 'On Acting and Non-Acting', in Zarilli, P. (ed) *Acting (Re)Considered*, London, Routledge.

Kitson, N. and Spiby, I. (1995) *Primary Drama Handbook*, London, Watts.

Kitson, N. and Spiby, I. (1997) *Drama 7-11: Developing Primary Teaching Skills*, London, Routledge.

Lawrence, C. (1982) 'Teacher and Role', *2D*, Volume 1, Number 2.

Lewicki,T. (1996) *From 'Play way' to 'Dramatic Art'*, Rome, LAS.

Lyotard, J.F. (1984) *The Postmodern Condition: A Report on Knowledge*, trans. Geoff Bennington and Brian Massumi. Manchester, Manchester University Press.

MacIntyre, A. (1981) *After Virtue*, London, Duckworth.

Mamet, D (1997) *True and False: Heresay and Common Sense for the Actor*, London, Faber and Faber.

McBurney, S. (1992) 'Theatre de Complicite', September 1st, The Late Show, BBC.

Mead, G. H. (1934) *Mind, Self and Society*, Chicago, University of Chicago Press.

Morgan, G. (ed) (1983) *Beyond Method*, London, Verso.

Morgan, N. and Saxton, J. (1989) *Teaching Drama: A Mind of Many Wonders*, Cheltenham, Hutchinson Educational.

National Council for Drama Training (1999) 'Criteria and procedures for Accreditation of Courses', November.

Neelands, J. (1990) *Structuring Drama Work*, Cambridge, Cambridge University Press.

Neelands, J. (1993) *Writing in Imagined Contexts*, Toronto, Research Services Toronto Board of Education.

Neelands, J. (1998) *Beginning Drama 11-14*, London, David Fulton.

Neelands, J. (2000) 'In the hands of living people' in *Drama Research*, Number 1.

Neelands, J. and Dobson,W. (2000) *Theatre Directions*, London, Hodder and Stoughton.

Nicholson, H. (1994) 'Drama and the Arts: From Polemic to Practice. Celebrating ourselves as Experts' in *Drama*, Volume 3, Number 1.

Nicholson, H. (1995) *NADIE journal*, Volume 19, Number 2

Nisbet, J. D. and Watt, J. (1980) *Case Study*. Rediguide 26, University of Nottingham, School of Education.

O'Conner, P. (2000) Book Review, Australia Drama *NADIE Journal*, Volume 24, Number 1.

O'Hanlon, C. (1993) 'The importance of an articulated theory of professional development' in J. Elliott (ed) *Reconstructing Teacher Education: Teacher Development*, London, Falmer.

O'Neill, C. (ed) (1984) *Dorothy Heathcote: Collected Writings on Education and Drama*, London, Hutchinson.

O'Neill, C. (1995a) *Drama Worlds: A Framework for Process Drama*, Portsmouth, New Hampshire, Heinemann.

O'Neill, C. (1995b) 'Pre-text: The Artistry of Cecily O'Neill' in Philip Taylor *op. cit.*

O'Neill, C., Lambert, A., Linnell, R. and Warr-Watd, J. (1976) *Drama Guidelines*, Heinemann, London.

O'Neill, C. and Lambert, A. (1982) *Drama Structures: A Practical Handbook for Teachers*, Hutchinson, London.

O'Neill, C. (1996) 'Into the Labyrinth: Theory and Research in Drama' in P. Taylor *op. cit.*

O'Toole, J. (1977) *Theatre in Education*, London, Hodder and Stoughton.

O'Toole, J. (1992) *The Process of Drama* (Negotiating Art and Meaning), London, Routledge.

O'Toole, J. (1996) 'Art in Scholarship and Scholarship in Art: Towards a Poetics of Drama Research' in P. Taylor *op. cit.*

O'Toole, J. (2001) Pilgrims' Progress, Paper delivered at IDEA World Conference of Drama/Theatre and Education, Bergen, Norway.

O'Toole, J. and Haseman, B. (1988) *Dramawise – An Introduction to GCSE Drama*, London, Heinemann.

Oddey, A. (1999) *Performing Women: Stand-Ups, Strumpets and Itinerants*, London, Macmillan.

Oida, Y. with Lorna Marshall (1992) *An Actor Adrift*, London, Methuen.

Okpewho, I. (ed) (1990) *The Oral Performance in Africa*, Ibadan, Spectrun Books.

Parkes, M. (1992) 'The Art of Pedagogy: Artistic Behaviour as a Model for Teaching', *Art Education*, Volume 45, Number 5.

Parks, K. (1995) 'You've been in a play, you teach the drama class': The need for a Standardised System for the Hiring of School Drama Teachers' in Juliana Saxton and Carole Miller (eds), *Canadian Tertiary Drama Education Perspectives on Practice*, Victoria, University of Victoria.

Pavis, P. (1985) 'Theatre Analysis: Some Questions and a Questionnaire' *New Theatre Quarterly*, 1(2).

Pears, D. (1971) *Wittgenstein*, London, Fontana.

Polanyi, M. (1958) *Personal Knowledge: towards a post-critical philosophy*, London, Routledge and Kegan Paul.

Poster, M. (ed) (1988) *Jean Baudrillard: Selected Writings*, Cambridge, Polity Press.

Pratt Cooney, M. (1997) 'Lehrstucke and Process Drama', *Drama Matters*, Volume 2, Number 1. pp41-52.

Propp, V. (1968) [1928] *Morphology of the Folktale*, trans., revised edition, Austen and London, University of Texas Press.

Read, A. (1993) *Theatre and Everyday Life*, London, Routledge.

Readman, G. and Lamont, G. (1994) *Drama – A Handbook for Primary Teachers*, London, Hodder and Stoughton

Redington, C. (1983) *Can Theatre Teach?* Oxford, Pergamon Press.

Richardson, H (1994) 'Genre, Gender and Play: Feminist Theory and Drama Education' in *NADIE Journal*, Volume 19, Number 2.

Richardson, V. (1994) 'Problems and possibilities of institutionalising teacher research' in Sandra Hollingsworth (ed) *Teacher Research and Educational Reform,* Chicago, National Society for the Study of Education.

Ritchie, R. (1987) *The Joint Stock Book: The Making of a Theatre Collective*, London, Methuen.

Robinson, K. (ed) (1980) *Exploring Theatre and Education*, London, Heinemann.

Romain, M. (1992) *A profile of Jonathan Miller*, Cambridge, Cambridge University Press.

Rothenberg, J. (1977) 'New Models, New Visions: Some Notes Toward a Poetics of Performance', in Michael Benamou and Charles Caramello (eds) *Performance in Postmodern Culture*, Madison: Coda Press Inc.

Roose-Evans, J. (1999) *Experimental Theatre from Stanislavsky to Peter Brook*, London, Routledge.

Rudlin, J. (1994) *Commedea dell'arte: An Actor's Handbook*, London, Routledge.

Sandford, M. R. (1995) *Happenings and Other Acts*, London, Routledge.

Saussure, F. (1966) *Course in General Linguistics*, trans. Wade Baskin, New York, McGraw-Hill Paperbacks.

Schechner, R. (1988) *Performance Theory*, London, Routledge.

Schechner, R. (1996) 'Worlds of Performance' editorial introduction to Part One in P. Zarrilli *op. cit.*

Schechner, R. (2002) *Performance Studies: An introduction*, London, Routledge.

Schutzman, M. and Cohen-Cruz, J. (eds) (1994) *Playing Boal: theatre, therapy, activism*, London, Routledge.

Selden, R. and Widdowson, P (1993) *Contemporary Literary Theory*, London, Harvester Wheatsheaf.

Sennett, R. (1977) *The Fall of Public Man, Cambridge*, Cambridge University Press.

Shakespeare, W. (1994) *Romeo and Juliet*, London, Penguin Popular Classics.

Shaw, F. (1999) cited in C. Zucker, *In the Company of Actors: Reflections on the Craft of Acting,* London, A & C Black.

Shaw, F. (2001) 'Best of Times: Worst of Times' *The Sunday Times Magazine*.

Shaw, G.B. (1957) *The Quintessence of Ibsenism*, New York, Hill and Wang.

Slade, P. (1958) *An Introduction to Child Drama*, London, University of London Press.

Smurthwaite, N. (2000) 'Hell Hath Number Fury' Stratford, RSC book.

Sophocles, (1958) *The Oedipus Plays of Sophocles,* trans. Paul Roche, New York, A Mentor Classic.

Stanislavsky, K. (1980) *An Actor Prepares*, translated by Elizabeth Reynolds, London, Eyre Methuen.

States, B.O. (1996) 'The Actor's Presence', in P. Zarrilli *op.cit.*

Strindberg, A. (1991) *Plays One, Strindberg*, London, Methuen.

Styan, J.L. (1975) *Drama, Stage and Audience*, Cambridge, Cambridge University Press.

Tauber, R.T. and Mester, C.S. (1994) *Acting Lessons for Teachers: Using Performance Skills in the Classroom.* Westport, Connecticut, Praeger.

Taylor, P (1996) *Researching Drama and The Arts Education: Paradigms and Possibilities*, London, Falmer Press.

Taylor, P. (1996) 'Rebellion, Reflective Turning and Arts Education Research' in P.Taylor *op.cit.*

Taylor, P. (2000) *The Drama Classroom: Action, Reflection, Transformation*, London, Routledge Falmer.

Toye, N. and Prendiville, N. (2000) *Drama and traditional story for the early years*, London, Routledge Falmer.

Tufnell, M and Crickmay, C (1993) *Body, Space, Image:Notes Towards Improvisation and Performance*, London, Dance Books.

Ubersfeld, A. (1978) *Lire le theatre*, Paris, Editions Sociales.

Vattimo, G. (1988) *The End of Modernity: Nihilism and Hermeneutics in Postmodern Culture*, Baltimore, John Hopkins University Press.

Veltrusky, J. (1964 [1940]) (trans.) 'Man and Object in the Theatre' in Garvin, P.L. *A Prague School Reader on Aesthetics, Literary Structure, and Style*, Washington, Georgetown University Press.

Wagner, B.J. (ed) (1998) *Educational Drama and Language Arts:What Research Shows*, Portsmouth, New Hampshire, Heinemann.

Wallace, J. (2000) 'A new stage in Greek Tragedy', *The Times Higher Education Supplement*, January 18th.

Watson, I. (1995) 'Reading' the actor: performance, presence, and the synesthetic' *New Theatre Quarterly*, Number 42, Volume xi. May.

Warren, B. (1995) *Creating a Theatre in Your Classroom.* North York, Ontario, Captus University Press.

Way, B (1967) *Developments through Drama*, Harlow, Longman.

Whatman, J. (1998) 'Educating Secondary Student Teachers Through Drama Education' in *NADIE journal*, Selected IDIERI papers,Volume 22, Number 1.

Wickham, G. (1967) *The Ferens Lecture*, The University of Hull.

Williams, P. and Chrisman, L.(ed) (1993) *Colonial Discourse and Post-Colonial Theory:A Reader,* Hemel Hempstead, Harvester Wheatsheaf.

Williams,T. (1977) *The Glass Menagerie*, Harmondsworth, Penguin Books.

Willis, E. and D'Arienzo, C. (1981) *Writing Scripts for Television and Radio*, Holt, Rhinehart and Winston.

Wilshire, B. (1991) *Role Playing and Identity:The Limits of Theatre as Metaphor*, Bloomington and Indianapolis, Indiana University Press.

Winston, J. (1998) *Drama, Narrative and Moral Education*, London, Falmer Press.

Winston, J. (1998) *Beginning Drama 4-11*, London, David Fulton.

Zarilli, P (ed) (1996) *Acting (Re)Considered. Theories and Practices,* London, Routledge.

Zola, E (1989) *Therese Raquin*, trans. Pip Broughton, Bath, Absolute Classics

Zucker, C (1999) *In the Company of Actors: Reflections on the Craft of Acting,* London, A & C Black.

Interviews

Simon Callow (2000) at Milton Keynes, UK

Cecily O'Neill (2000) in London, UK

John O'Toole (1999) in Brisbane, Australia

Fiona Shaw (2000) in Dublin, Ireland

Performances

Goosebumps (1999), Peepolikus, Roadmender, Northampton.

The Mystery of Charles Dickens (2000), Milton Keynes Theatre.

Medea (2000), The Abbey Theatre, Dublin and Queens Theatre, London.

King Lear (1997) (with Kathryn Hunter), The Young Vic Theatre, London.

The Lady in the Van (2000) (with Maggie Smith) Queen's Theatre, London.

Hedda (1975) (with Glenda Jackson) Brut Productions, Hollywood Nites.

Hedda Gabler (1993) (with Fiona Shaw) BBC.

Mobbs' Boys, Theatre in Education tour, Northamptonshire 1985

Index